THE LIFE OF TOM HORN REVISITED

Doyce B. Nunis, Jr.

THE WESTERNERS
LOS ANGELES CORRAL

THE LIFE OF TOM HORN REVISITED

Copyright © 1992 by Doyce B. Nunis, Jr.
All Rights Reserved

Published by Los Angeles Corral - Westerners
Los Angeles, California 90027 U.S.A.

Library of Congress Catalog Card No. 92-29878
I.S.B.N. No. 0-87095-107-6

Library of Congress Cataloging-in-Publication Data

Nunis, Doyce Blackman.
    The life of Tom Horn revisited / Doyce B. Nunis, Jr.
        p.   cm. — (Keepsake / the Westerners, Los Angeles Corral;
    no. 30)
    Includes bibliographical references and index.
    ISBN 0-87095-107-6
    1. Horn, Tom, 1860-1903.   2. Apache Indians—Wars, 1883-1886.
3. Frontier and pioneer life—West (U.S.)   4. West (U.S.)—
Biography.   5. Scouts and scouting—Southwest, New—Biography.
6. Trials (Murder)—Wyoming—Cheyenne.   I. Title.   II. Series:
Keepsake (Westerners. Los angeles Corral); no. 30.
E83.88.H676N86   1992
973.8'4'092—dc20   92-29878
[B]   CIP

THE WESTERNERS
LOS ANGELES CORRAL
P.O. Box 80250
San Marino, California • 91118-8250

Table of Contents

Horn's Family; Early Youth; Cowboy Days; Farmer and Miner; Hired Gun; To the Southwest; Overland Mail Employee; U.S. Army Herder; Meets Al Sieber; Army/Apache Conflict; Life Among the Coyotero Apache; Working for Tully, Ochoa & DeLong; Battle of Cibicu Creek; Attack on Fort Apache; Chief Loco Breakout; Tupper-Loco Fight; Battle of Middle Mountain; Encounter with Mexican Troops; General Crook's Second Apache Campaign; Surrender of Geronimo; Geronimo Breakout; Tracking Geronimo; Fateful Encounter, the Death of Captain Crawford; Geronimo Surrenders, Then Flees; General Miles Assumes Command; Horn, Chief of Scouts; Search for Geronimo South of the Border; Geronimo Surrenders to Lieutenant Gatewood; Apaches Exiled to Florida; Horn Returns to Civilian Life; Notes.

Mining Near Tombstone; Punching Cattle; Pleasant Valley War; Deputy Sheriff; Sets Rodeo Record; Buffalo Bill Cody Offers Job; Assists "Doc" Shores in Arrest; Agent for the Pinkerton Detective Agency; Tracking Jim McCabe; Arrested for Robbery in Reno; First Trial, Hung Jury; Second Trial, Acquittal; Pinkerton Man; Johnson County War; Cowboy Sleuth; Wyoming Stock Growers' Association Employee; Independent Cattle Detective; Spanish American War; Back to Wyoming; Meets Miss Kimmell; Miller-Nickell Feud; Willie Nickell's Murder; Coble Employee; Range Conflict; Marshall LeFors Enters the Case; Suspects Horn; LeFors Lays a Trap; The Trap Is Sprung; Horn's "Confession;" Arrested; Charged With Murder of Willie Nickell; Horn's Defense Team; Trial Begins; Question of Miss Kimmell; Defense and Evidence Pondered; Horn Takes the Stand; Summation for the Defense; The Prosecution Thunders; Guilty Verdict; Defense Appeals; Appeal Denied; Clemency Hearing; Governor Chatterton Refuses; Horn's Last Days; Execution and Burial; Flaws in the Case; Friends Defend Horn; Damned by Critics; Friends Rebut; Charlie Siringo's Vendetta; William Pinkerton Doubts Horn's Guilt; Horn and the Apaches on Film and TV; The Horn Enigma; Notes.

Preface

In 1986, I was asked by R.R. Donnelley & Sons, Chicago, to prepare the 1987 *Lakeside Classic* for them. Aficionados of history of the American West are well acquainted with this distinguished series of books which began publication in 1903 and has continued without interruption to this day. The *Classics* are an annual publication, always published at Christmas time, and are sent gratis to clients, employees, learned institutions, and select individuals who are lucky enough to be on the approved mailing list. They are the company's yearly present; none are sold on the commercial market. Copies of the *Classics* that do appear for sale on the antiquarian book market come from the libraries of individuals who have been recipients of copies or else have purchased them when available.

Each *Lakeside Classic* conforms to a specific set of criteria. It must be a first-person narrative written from first-hand knowledge; it must be historical in content and focus, and it must relate to some aspect of the history of the United States. The material in question should be a long out-of-print book, usually in the public domain, meaning the copyright has expired. Lastly, it should make for good and informed reading. To insure accuracy and reliability, each *Lakeside Classic* is edited by a person with solid credentials, usually an authority in the subject field of the text to be reprinted. For many years this was Milo M. Quaife. Current practice is to match an historian with expertise in the narrative's content. An added modern touch is the inclusion of illustrations and one or more maps where deemed appropriate.

The book I was commissioned to edit for the 1987 *Lakeside Classic* was the *Life of Tom Horn, Government Scout and Interpreter Written by Himself: A Vindication.* This was originally published in 1904 by the Louthan Book Company, Denver. The autobiography was edited by Horn's friend and employer, John C. Coble. The text of that edition was used for the 1987 *Lakeside Classic* edition. However, the latter omitted Coble's preface and the concluding appendix, "Supplementary Articles." These were deemed superfluous and, so, were not included.

In 1964, the University of Oklahoma Press reprinted the entire first edition under the same title, with an introduction by Dean F. Krakel, a trained historian and archivist, who had a deep interest in Horn. His abiding fascination led to the publication in 1954 of *The Saga of Tom Horn,* a book that was called "A thorough study of the trial and execution of Tom Horn" by the foremost Western American bibliographer, Ramon F. Adams.

In editing the third publication of Horn's autobiography in 1987, as editor I made several editorial intrusions. First, in a number of places in the original 1904 edition, personal and place names and/or words were misspelled. In some instances, these were obvious typographical errors; in others, words had been spelled phonetically. It should be remembered that Horn had only a minimal elementary school education. All these were corrected.

Second, the original manuscript contained no chapters, let alone chapter headings. Therefore, Coble took it upon himself to break the manuscript into chapters and to supply rather long Victorian-era headings. When Krakel prepared the 1964 reprint edition, which was not textually edited, he dropped Coble's chapter headings and used more simplified ones. The 1987 edition followed a similar editorial policy and included new, shorter chapter titles.

Lastly, the 1987 edition was edited for errors of fact and chronology, for Horn's memory was not reliable in all details. In addition, where needed, footnotes offered explanation or supportive data for the narrative. To complement the text, two indices were prepared, "A Biographical Directory" and "A Directory of Military Posts and Reservations." Also, an index was provided, something not to be found in the two previous editions.

While working on the 1987 edition, I became fascinated with Tom Horn. He struck me as an individual who obviously had some profound psychological problems. He most assuredly had an inferiority complex. To compensate for that serious flaw, he became a braggart and an outright liar. Indeed, it could be said, with some slight reservation, that he was a pathological liar who was unable to distinguish truth from fantasy. Not that he meant any harm, far from it. He was not given to character assassination like many a modern-day politician. But Horn could not resist making himself appear bigger than his life actually was. He was given to gross personal puffery. Yet, his autobiography contains a lot of solid historical information that can be found nowhere else.

As I pondered this situation, I decided to write a treatment of the *Life of Tom Horn* in an effort to sort out fact and fiction, and, at the same time, to provide a solid profile of the man and his life. To achieve that end, I divided his life into two parts, each of which is self-explanatory. I will say no more. I leave it to you, the reader, to decide whether or not Tom Horn's *Life* is a lie, or whether it has sufficient reliability to be treated as fact. What will your verdict be?

Los Angeles, California   Doyce B. Nunis, Jr.

May 1992

From Childhood

1

to Chief of Scouts

Mention the name Tom Horn to any knowledgeable historian or history buff of the American West and you will be guaranteed a ready response. Some will proclaim the man as a legend in his own time, the victim of a flawed judicial system. Others will belie such an assertion with equal vigor, holding that the man was nothing more than a hired gun, who finally got his just deserts when he was hung as a self-confessed murderer of a rancher's 14-year-old son. Horn's reputation is either damned or praised; there is no middle ground.

That such would be the fate of this child born on November 21, 1860, and named for his father, would have been quickly dismissed without further thought being given to such a fanciful idea. Surely, this never would have entered the minds of Horn's two older brothers, Charles and Martin, nor his four sisters, Nancy, Hannah, Maude, and Alice.[1] His siblings were destined to lead ordinary, uneventful lives as husbands, wives, and parents. But not Tom.

Tom was born on the family farm located in northeastern Missouri near Memphis, in Scotland County. His was an ordinary babyhood and childhood. His mother, a member of the Disciples of Christ, sometimes called Campbellites after the founder, Alexander Campbell (1788-1866) of Virginia, saw to it that he attended "church and Sunday school, as did most of the boys and girls in the neighborhood." But Tom found a way around that stricture. Early on, he became a good hunter. He would "steal out the gun and take the dog and hunt all day Sunday and many a night through the week, knowing full well that whenever I showed up at home I would get a whipping or scolding from my mother or a regular thumping from father." His bent for hunting, so that he could pursue his youthful passion, often led to his truancy from school.[2]

Tom Horn.

Courtesy Wyoming State Museum, Cheyenne.

Tom Horn's mother.

When Tom entered his teens, there was increasing conflict between him and his iron-willed father. A final clash, ending with a dreadful beating, resulted in the young 14-year-old striking out on his own. He fled the family farm; first for Kansas City; then on to Newton, Kansas, where he landed a job as a railroad construction worker. After less than a month's labor, he joined a bunch of Texas drovers who had trailed a herd of range cattle to the railroad for shipment east.[3] Without a doubt, the young teenager possessed a winning personality, a character feature that would thread through his life.

This initial range training was honed when he participated in the next trail drive to the Dodge City railhead. During those unrecorded years, since Horn makes no mention of them in his autobiography, the freshman cowboy became an expert at horsemanship and wrangling cattle, skills that remained with him to the end. In addition, he had an aptitude for languages which helped him to acquire a good speaking knowledge of Spanish from his *vaquero* cohorts, a talent that came in handy when Horn headed out on his own into the Southwest.

A fateful event, perhaps a portent of things to come, compelled his hurried departure from Texas. While preparing for another cattle drive, Horn and some of his friends, who had overindulged in drink, took off on a shooting spree, using as a target a newly whitewashed outhouse. Sometime later a mother and her little daughter were found dead in a nearby arroyo, innocent victims of the drunken cowboys' escapade. Tom did not wait for the law; he hightailed it northward.[4]

He made his way to the Flint Hills of Kansas and the small ranch of his brother, Charley. They soon decided to go partners, but sold out after a short tenure. About the same time (the year was 1878) Father Horn persuaded them to take a lease on some land he had at Burrton. But, for Tom, farm life was alien to what was clearly emerging as a personality trait: his restlessness. He had to be on the move.[5]

Hearing of the Leadville gold strike in the Colorado Territory, Tom took to the trail again. But dreams of striking it rich failed him as it did so many goldseekers. To sustain himself Tom became a section hand with a gun in the infamous Royal Gorge struggle between two hotly contending railroad companies anxious to secure the route as a monopoly. That experience seeded Tom's gunmanship. Then, once again, he turned to mining, but luck was against him. Disgruntled, with winter coming on, he decided to take the Santa Fe Trail to an unknown future.[6] Now standing six feet one inch tall, lean and muscular, the 19-year-old was ready for his manhood.

After reaching Santa Fe around Christmas in 1879, he found employment the following January with the Overland Mail route that ran from Santa Fe to Prescott, Arizona. For a couple of months, he drove the Overland stage from Santa Fe to Los Pinos. The pay was $50 a month. He was then transferred to the segment from Los Pinos to Bacon Springs or Crane's Ranch. In May, he was summoned by the superintendent to take some mules to Beaver Head Station, located close to the Verde River in Arizona, to replace those which had been stolen by Indians. By this time, Tom "could speak Mexican fairly well." As he remarked, "My feelings were so different and my life was so different from what it was at home that it semed as though I had been all my life on a stage line." [7]

After reaching Beaver Head, Tom struck out on his own for Camp Verde looking for new employment. That fall he "went to work . . .herding oxen at night for the men hauling wood into Camp Verde." He quickly earned the reputation as one of "the best night herders." The pay was an improvement too, $75 a month. When the three-month job ended, Tom headed for Prescott boasting, "I could speak Mexican as well as a native could."[8]

Upon reaching Prescott, he was hired by the U.S. Army Quartermaster to herd horses that had been brought overland from California for service in the Arizona Territory. He was made boss of the operation, his underlings being two Mexican drovers. The horses had to be herded until the various military posts sent in requisitions for replacement mounts. Their disbursement quickly followed, and Tom once again found himself

Al Sieber, Chief of Scouts, as he appeared in 1877, five years
before he met Tom Horn and employed him as an army packer.
Courtesy Arizona Historical Society.

without gainful employment.

It was at this juncture that fate stepped in. He supposedly met Al Sieber, who dropped in to Camp Verde from Fort Whipple. Impressed with Tom's ability to speak Spanish, Sieber recruited him as a "Mexican interpreter at $75.00 a month." Sieber told Horn that he "would be with him all the time, and [Horn] was tickled to get a chance to go. . . ."[9] They headed south for the San Carlos Agency. Thus, Tom Horn's subsequent career, as an army packer and later as a scout, was launched.

Sieber, a German immigrant, was born in the farm hamlet of Mingolsheim on the Kraich River, about midway between Heidelberg and Karlsruhe, in February 1844. Following the lead of a much older brother, Sieber's widowed mother took her brood and immigrated to Lancaster, Pennsylvania. With the advent of the Civil War, Sieber enlisted in the Union cause and was twice wounded at Gettysburg.

His westering is a long story. Suffice it to say that he made it to California, but eventually found his final home in the Arizona Territory in 1868, when lured to the environs of Prescott with visions of riches to be had in the newly discovered mines. Although he continued mining activities on and off for most of his Arizona days, his success was modest at best. His true claim to fame was his uncanny abilities and talents as a scout for the U.S. Army, an association begun in 1870, which lasted two decades. What made Sieber so special was his mastery of the Apache and Spanish languages. In the main, he served his 20-year tenure at the San Carlos Reservation.

During his scouting days, Sieber reputedly was wounded 28 times, including a badly wounded left foot which he sustained in an encounter with a small group of renegade Indians led by his former protege, the Apache Kid, on June 1, 1887, a wound that never completely healed. Despite his many wounds, it was age and the physical side effects of a hard life in the saddle that took its toll, forcing him to relinquish active field duty in 1885. Under a cloud of charges, he was dismissed abruptly from San Carlos in 1890. His twilight years were spent in mining, hunting thieves, and working for railroad and road construction companies. The latter employment cost him his life: he was killed in a rock slide while supervising Apache workers on a road construction job near Roosevelt Dam on the Salt River, February 19, 1907.[10]

It was Sieber who recruited and trained Horn in the techniques of scouting. Tom later recorded their fateful meeting at Camp Verde just after he had lost his job as a drover of cavalry horses for the Army. Shortly after, the two men headed for the San Carlos Reservation, thus launching a lifelong friendship. As Horn later declared: "Sieber was one the grandest men in the world in my eyes, and although old and white-headed and a cripple for life now, he is still a nobleman."[11]

In his autobiography, Tom places himself in Santa Fe near Christmas in 1874. This would have been when he was 14 years old. This is patently not the case. He then goes to work for the Overland Stage Company as a driver! Where did he learn that skill? He literally omits from his narrative, or jumbles, a full seven years of his life, 1874-1880.

But more. He writes that he met Al Sieber for the first time in July 1876 at Camp Verde. This would make him 15 years old. In 1904, Sieber, in a statement dated April 7, wrote categorically: "Tom went to work for me in the government pack train in 1882; he was with me and worked steady for me for three years. A more faithful or better worker or a more honorable man I never met in my life."[12] Most likely they actually met in the early spring of 1882, certainly not July 1876. The latter must be rejected without further comment.

Putting aside the grossly mistaken chronology, the focal point of Horn's Arizona years was the difficult and perplexing struggle the United States Army faced in securing the Southwest from hostile Apaches. On that frontier, the Army fought its last Indian war. It had a very formidable adversary in the nomadic, warlike Apaches, whose homeland encompassed the northern states of Mexico, principally Sonora and Chihuahua, the lower eastern part of Arizona, and all but the northwest quadrant of New Mexico.

To understand the Army/Apache conflict, one must keep in mind the diversity among the Apaches, a diversity set on clan or group lines and geographical dispersion, wherein loyalty to a chief or leader transcended tribalhood. Indeed, this prevailing characteristic led to inter-tribal or group conflict, a division that worked advantageously for the Army in its almost constant effort to bring hostile Apaches to heel.

Of all the Apache tribes, the best known was the Chiricahua. They were divided into three geographically defined groups: eastern, southern, and central. The eastern group was sub-divided into Warm Springs, Mimbrenos, or Mogollones Apaches. They looked upon southwestern New Mexico as their homeland. Two of their chiefs, Nana and Loco, were dominant figures during Horn's active scouting days. The southern group, the Pinery Apaches, had, as their dominant leaders, Geronimo and Juh, both very well known to Horn. Their lands comprised northern Sonora and Chihuahua. The central group called southeastern Arizona home and produced one famous chief, Cochise.

The Chiricahuas were quite distinctive because they were nomadic, non-agricultural Indians. It was mainly the increased competition for food, brought about by the influx of Spanish and Americans to their area, that caused them to become superior horsemen and fierce warriors. Yet, their freewheeling ways alienated many of their fellow Apaches, and their murderous raids against the white settlers earned them an abiding and deep-seated hatred. So much so that Mexicans and Americans alike had little or no compunction in seeing an Apache dead, especially a Chiricahua.

Warlike actions between the Apaches and Americans flared in 1863 when gold was discovered on Apache land. It would be an off-and-on confrontation which lasted until 1886. The reasons for these 23 years of conflict stemmed from the building of roads for stagecoaches and later railroads; the never-ending mining strikes; the ever-present border criminal element; plus irresponsible Indian agency mismanagement. Not to be forgotten are tragic episodes that fed the flames of racial hatred, notably the infamous Camp Grant Massacre of April 28, 1871, which resulted in the deaths of 144 Apaches. In the bargain, frontier bullies preyed remorselessly on any hapless Apache they came across. Apaches retaliated in kind by attacking vulnerable travelers, isolated ranches, and small army detachments.

A semblance of peace and serenity was finally forged by Brigadier General George Crook in 1875 during his first tour of duty as commander of the Department of Arizona. He won the respect and confidence of the hostiles which enabled him to achieve the placement of the Apaches on the San Carlos Reservation. That resettlement began to lay the basis for what might be called the "peace and blanket factions" among the Apaches. As a result, if "blanket" Indians, meaning those in favor of warfare, jumped the reservation on more than one occasion, the peace-prone Apaches were easily recruited as army scouts to seek out the renegades. Indeed, the majority of the army scouts were Apaches who had no love for the warlike Chiricahuas.

When Horn arrived in Arizona during the late spring of 1880, Army/Apache relations were peaceful, other than a few renegade "blanket" Indians roving the countryside. Tom decided to spend the 1881-1882 winter with a Coyotero Apache band led by Pedro, an old, peace-loving chief, but he departed in the spring. In Pedro's village, Tom learned the Apache ways and language. That experience was to prove invaluable in his service to the Army, which began in the spring of 1882, when scouts were recruited from old Pedro's village and Horn, then at age 20, became an army packer. By the summer, some Chiricahuas had broken out from their reservation and were back on the warpath. The situation worsened. Crook was later recalled to again try to achieve the surrender of the warring Chiricahuas and restore peace to the bloodied southwestern frontier.

Horn's recollection of his activities, after his arrival in Santa Fe, are unreliable. Since he could not have met Sieber and been associated with him in 1876, the dates suggested below are probably more correct. Because he says he became a herder, where did he learn such a skill? By neglecting his cowboy training in Texas and on a trail drive, he leads the reader to believe he simply picked it up as he worked along. Hardly! If he was as experienced as he said he was, then he had to have had, at a minimum, a couple of years training on the range.

Old Chief Pedro of the Coyotero Apache. Horn spent the winter
of 1881-1882 in his encampment where he learned the Apache
language and customs. *Courtesy D'Arcy Indian Center, Newberry
Library, Chicago.*

As for his stay with the Coyoteros led by old Chief Pedro, and since
there was such a chief, this, then, must be accepted as fact for Horn did
learn Apache. He must have gotten his start learning the language during
his residence among the Coyotero. It may well be that he came to Arizona
in the spring of 1880, thus he could have spent the winter of 1881-1882 with
old Pedro's band. Yet, he infers that he actually spent the winter of 1876
among the Apache.[13] Since this is rooted in his supposed July 1876 meeting
with Sieber, this, too, must be discounted as erroneous. The supposition of
this writer is that it would appear more correct to suggest that Horn spent
the winter of 1881-1882 living with the Apaches.

Perhaps the more accurate chronology for Horn would be as follows.
He came to Arizona in the spring of 1880. He then went to work for three
months as a herder, taking the job sometime after May. When that job was
completed, he was employed herding horses for the Army. He boldly
states that at the age of 16 he was made boss of the operation. A likely tale,
indeed! What were his credentials?

In his autobiography, there is probably an element of truth when he
records the fact that in the fall of 1879 he went to Tucson and was
employed by the firm of Tully, Ochoa & DeLong Company. It would have

been a perfect lead to a meeting with Al Sieber since Horn was posted to the San Carlos Reservation in the spring of the following year to handle the distribution of cattle supplied by that company to the agency.[14] Obviously, a splendid opportunity to meet Sieber who was stationed there. Again, this, too, is unlikely because of the dates.

So, if one reconstructs the chronology more logically, it would appear that Horn probably worked for the Army as a herder of horses in the fall of 1880. When that job was completed, he was employed by the Tucson firm of Tully, Ochoa & DeLong. That being the case, he served, beginning in the spring of 1881, at the San Carlos Reservation. There he met one of the Coyotero, Mickey Free, a young brave more or less Tom's age, who induced him to come and live amongst his people led by Chief Pedro. Thus, Horn spent the winter of 1881-1882 among the Apache. Come the spring of 1882, he meets Sieber and gets his first army job with him as a packer just in time to be a part of the expeditionary force sent out to intercept the breakout of Chief Loco and his followers.

Mickey Free, Coyotero Apache, army scout, and interpreter. A member of Chief Pedro's band, he was instrumental in arranging for Horn to winter among his people. *Courtesy Arizona Historical Society.*

Horn in his autobiography tells us much of Brigadier General Crook's second-command tenure in the Department of Arizona. For most of that tour of duty, Tom worked as a packer for the Army and was extremely adept at that job. Confirmation of this is not hard to find. Crook resumed command September 4, 1882. One of his brilliant contributions to the military pursuit of the nomadic Chiricahuas, who usually fled south to sanctuary in Mexico, was to introduce pack trains into the chase so that army cavalry would have greater mobility and maneuverability in the field. But this took skilled packers to quickly ready the supply train so that it would keep up with the army units to be serviced and minimize any misadventures.[15]

Discounting all of Horn's story which threads his life with that of Al Sieber, 1876-1882, we must conclude, based on the evidence supplied by that famed Chief of Scouts, that his association with Horn commenced sometime in 1882, possibly the spring of that year. At that time, Horn became a packer, not a scout nor an intimate of Sieber's. It is obvious, however, that he came to his job well-equipped as a herder, cowboy, and packer, as well as an experienced trail hand, in addition to his linguistic skills, Spanish and Apache.

But Horn would have us believe instead that he was employed as an army translator at $100 a month, a position he states he received in the spring 1880![16] Not once does he ever mention one word about being a mule packer! Yet, this was most assuredly his job until at least 1885. As Sieber declared in 1904, Tom worked for him as an army packer for three years, beginning in 1882!

In the face of that established fact, Horn embroiders one of his most fanciful tales around Geronimo and Sieber. He tells us that in the spring of 1880, Chief Nana, a close confidant and companion to Victoria, made it known that Geronimo, then living in Mexico, desired to move to the San Carlos Reservation. Taking advantage of this opportunity, Sieber, accompanied by Horn, at least so he says, traveled to the appointed rendezvous in the Terras Mountains for a parley. At the meeting, because Geronimo spoke Apache too fast for Sieber, Horn was called upon to translate! After an eloquent appeal by Sieber to the Indians to return to Arizona, the council ended. A large number of older and younger Indians decided to follow Sieber back across the border to live on the reservation. For much of the remainder of that year, 1880, Horn was busy escorting those Indians who opted for life at the agency from Mexico to San Carlos. This is pure poppycock. Horn was not with Sieber. However, it is true that Sieber did

Geronimo, feared Chiricahua warrior, who terrorized southern Arizona and New Mexico territories until 1886. *Courtesy Arizona Historical Society.*

undertake such a mission, one which did prove successful.[17]

By June 1880, with so many Indians leaving the wilds for life on the reservation, according to Horn, "scouts and interpreters were again all discharged and fired off the reservation. Appropriations had run out and the Quartermaster had no money to pay [them]." Tom headed for Tucson. There he was employed by Tully, Ochoa & DeLong.

Beginning in July 1880 and for the ensuing year, Tom was employed at the handsome salary of $150 a month to handle the distribution end at San Carlos. Early on Tom spotted two problems. First, the Indians appeared to run the reservation to suit themselves, including helping themselves to the cattle without prior payment to the government. Second, he spotted the fact that the San Carlos agent, Joseph C. Tiffany, "was so busy selling the Indians' rations to freighters, prospectors and to merchants in Globe and McMinnerville, that the Indian troubles didn't seem to worry him very much." Indeed, Tiffany was subsequently indicted by a federal grand jury, October 24, 1882. Protesting his innocence, he was never brought to trial.[18]

By taking this stance in his autobiography, Horn positions himself as a prospective participant in the tragic fight at Cibicu (sometimes Cibecue) Creek, an encounter that took place on August 30, 1881. On that date, Colonel Eugene A. Carr, commanding a contingent of 79 troopers and six officers from Fort Apache, accompanied by 23 Apache scouts, arrested a young Apache medicine man name Noch-ay-del-klinne, who resided on Cibicu Creek. The medicine man had a large following among the reservation Indians and was a precursor of the more famed Ghost Dance craze of 1890. He, too, held that the great Apache warrior chiefs, who had been slain in battle, would rise from the dead and help the Apaches to liberate their land from the stranglehold of the white man.[19]

With the medicine man arrested, the next day Carr's detachment commenced the return to Fort Apache. But the news of the arrest of the famed medicine man had spread quickly, and Indians began gathering in the vicinity. Gunfire broke out. When the firing commenced, Carr immediately ordered the medicine man killed, and it was done. Some of the Army/Apache scouts defected on the spot and were reputedly responsible for the death of Captain Edmund C. Hentig, two troopers, and Hentig's orderly. Another two seriously wounded cavalrymen died subsequently. It was a costly failure which resulted from the treachery of the defecting Indian sergeants. Although these scout mutineers were later rounded up, brought to trial, and convicted, two of them being hung for their part in

Colonel Eugene A. Carr who commanded at the Battle of Cibicu
Creek. *Courtesy Arizona Historical Society.*

the death of Hentig, this tragic incident meant only one thing—open
warfare.[20]

On September 1, 1881, the Indians boldly attacked Fort Apache. But the
attack was rebuffed due to the return of Colonel Carr's detachment on the
afternoon of August 31. They were on hand to help repel the attackers the
next day. Fortunately, only one American officer was wounded; in
addition, Carr's mount was shot from under him. Quickly reinforcements
were summoned to Fort Apache to press the advantage of fending off the
hostiles. By October 1, Colonel Ronald S. Mackenzie succeeded Carr as
commander of the District of Apache, a command augmented by
additional troops under the command of Colonel Luther P. Bradley.[21]

Horn, as one might suspect, has himself playing a major role in the fight
at Cibicu Creek. Not only that, he also has Sieber present. Horn's fanciful
story has Sieber and himself leading the Indian scouts to Cibicu to arrest
five troublesome Indians. He makes no mention of the medicine man who
was the motivating reason for the Carr expedition's mission! More impor-
tantly, Sieber, himself, was not involved in the fight at Cibicu Creek.[22]

Fort Apache, Arizona Territory, in 1884 during the height of the Army/Apache conflict. *Courtesy Arizona Historical Society.*

William C. Barnes, who at the time was an army sergeant and telegraph operator at Fort Apache, later declared, with some vehemence:

> ...[Horn's] long yarn in his book telling of his presence at the battle of Cibecue is an outrageous, bareface lie from start to finish. I knew every soldier, officer, packer and scout that took part in the fight. I saw the command leave Fort Apache and met it four or five miles west of the .post the afternoon they returned from the unfortunate affair. Tom Horn was not with the command at any time....[23]

So much for another hyperbolical story.

In the aftermath of the death of the Apache medicine man, the countryside was thrown into terror by marauding Apaches. A number of ranchers and ill-fated travelers paid the ultimate price. But such deaths only spurred the Army to push forward with a punitive campaign, one that was launched with as much dispatch as the cavalry could muster. It was in this expeditionary force, in 1882, that Tom Horn finally made his army debut, not as a translator, not as a scout, but as a mule packer.

23

A major turn of events occurred in March 1882. The sly Apache leader, Juh, traveled north from his Mexico sanctuary with a deliberate plan. His intent was direct: to precipitate another major Apache uprising by forcing Loco, "a wise and venerable former lieutenant of Victoria, a man who inclined towards peace," to break reservation with his followers, some 700 strong, reputedly at rifle point. The plan came to fruition on April 19 when Loco and his followers broke out and made for Mexico. The breakout cost the life of Albert D. Sterling, chief of the San Carlos police, and an Indian policeman, Sagotal, both gunned down by Juh's renegades.[24]

Immediately, news of the breakout spurred an army response. Several contingents of cavalry were dispatched to head off the fleeing Indians, who, because of their large number, were moving slowly south toward Mexico. Setting out for the border, Loco's band followed the Gila River. At Steins Peak Range the pursuing cavalry engaged the Indians, but failed to press their advantage, much to the disgust of Al Sieber acting as Chief of Scouts. The Indians retired through Doubtful Canyon, then crossed the San Simon Valley toward Galeyville and Cave Creek in the Chiricahua Mountains. Loco's band then recrossed the valley to Skeleton Canyon and went over the Peloncillo Range to Cloverdale and from there, finally, across the border into Mexico.[25]

**Chief Loco whose breakout from the San Carlos Reservation
with his followers led to the Battle of Middle Mountain in which
he was soundly defeated and brought back to the reservation.**
Courtesy D'Arcy Indian Center, Newberry Library.

Lieutenant Colonel George A. Forsythe who commanded the U.S. Army cavalry at the Battle of Middle Mountain which defeated Chief Loco and his followers. *Courtesy Arizona Historical Society.*

Some 20 miles south of the border, not suspecting that the American army cavalry had pressed on in their wake, the Apaches stopped to recoup and celebrate their safe arrival in Mexico near Sierra Media (Middle Mountain). There Sieber tracked them and boldly scouted their encampment without detection. He then guided the American force from the 6th Cavalry, under Captains Tullius C. Tupper and William C. Rafferty, 107 men in all, with senior officer Tupper commanding, into position for a two-pronged surprise attack on the Apache camp. Combat was enjoined on April 28, 1882. When hostilities ceased, 14 Apaches were slain and 74 horses captured, the latter a serious blow to Loco for he was practically dismounted. The encounter was dubbed the Tupper-Loco fight. On April 29, reinforcements under the command of Colonel George A. Forsyth, consisting of seven troops of cavalry and two or three companies of scouts, joined Tupper's camp in the evening. Command now devolved to Forsyth as senior officer.[26]

That same day, Colonel Lorenzo Garcia, a seasoned Mexican frontier Indian fighter, commanding the 6th Regiment of Chihuahua cavalry, plus augmented troops from the 4th Regiment and some local guard or militia troops, hit the Indians south of Arroyo Carreta, not far from where Aliso Creek empties into it. The Indians sustained heavy casualties; a number of women and children were taken captive.

The following day, the American forces, in the ongoing hit-and-run battle, pressed forward only to encounter the Mexican contingent under Garcia. Immediately, Garcia informed Forsyth that he was in violation of Mexican sovereignty by trespassing on Mexican soil. A prickly confrontation ensued. Luckily, it was resolved by the bluff of Forsyth and the timidity of Garcia, neither of whom wished an armed response leading to bloodshed. Garcia made no effort to intervene when the American cavalry turned back north, headed for the international border.[27]

In his autobiography, Horn casts himself in the role of a scout and sidekick of Sieber, right in the forefront of the action. Sieber, who wrote detailed accounts of the chase and clash at Middle Mountain, makes no mention of Horn at all. Yet, Horn's story of the Tupper-Loco chase and fight is surprisingly accurate, particularly as to the route of flight and pursuit, and his account of the actual fight, as well as the confrontation with the Mexican forces, is very close to the actual facts. This leads to the obvious conclusion that Horn was a part of the expeditionary force and was an actual witness to these events, but not as a scout and bosom companion of Sieber. At most, Horn was a packer with the support mule train and witnessed the events from the rear ranks as they unfolded.

By the summer of 1882, southern Arizona was plagued by various bands of raiding hostile Apache. Mounting civilian deaths provoked increased public pressure on the Army for swift and determined action to curb the murdering renegades. Sentiment was heavily critical of the Army's ineffectual efforts to control the situation. Alarm became greater in early July when the Cibicu insurgents, under the leadership of Na-ti-o-tish, numbering some 40 fighting warriors, broke out from San Carlos. John L. Colvig, the chief of police who had replaced the slain Sterling, and three of his Indian policemen were killed. An army offensive was quickly mounted.[28]

Eleven companies of troops drawn from Forts Apache, McDowell, Verde, and others, took to the field to intercept and capture the renegades. The fugitive Apaches laid an ambush for the pursuing cavalry in the Tonto Basin where the trail climbs over the Mongollon Rim. Fortunately, Sieber discovered the trap and the prospect of ambush gave way to an army attack on July 17. The encounter at Big Dry Wash Creek, near General's Spring on Chevelon's Fork or East Clear Creek, was a decisive defeat for the renegades. Their leader and over a score of adherents were killed; the rest were made captive. Captain Adna R. Chaffee received accolades for leading this highly successful operation.[29]

Horn was a witness and, mayhap, a participant in the Battle of Big Dry

Wash, or Chevelon's Fork as he called it. He supposedly recruited a band of Apache volunteers from the Coyoteros to aid the punitive expedition. More likely, Horn was with Sieber as a mule packer, at best, since translators were not really needed for this particular military venture. At the successful conclusion of the operation, Horn returned to Fort Apache.[30]

In his autobiography, Horn brags about a highly complimentary letter he received from Colonel Orlando B. Willcox, the department commander, praising him for his heroism at "Tupper's Battle Ground at the Sierra Enmedio in Mexico," where he carried a wounded sergeant to safety, "and also for saving the balance of the command after Captain Hentig had been killed on Cibicu. . . [and] also for my excellent service with my volunteer force from Pedro's camp" at the Battle of Chevelon's Fork. Ironically, Horn is claiming credit due more properly to Sieber. He may well have saved "old Sergeant Murray" at the Tupper-Loco fight, but certainly his role at Cibicu and Chevelon's Fork are exaggerated to say the least.[31]

Nor can Horn restrain himself in respect to inflating his own importance. In his autobiography, he elevates himself into the same class as Sieber, even being asked to testify before army officials about the incursion of Forsyth's command into Mexico in pursuit of Loco and his followers. His fantasies, regarding this, are amusing at best.[32]

It was at this juncture of the Army/Apache conflict that Washington decided to return Brigadier General George Crook to the command of the Arizona Department. Since once before he had brought order to chaos in the department, he appeared to be the only officer capable of doing it a second time. He took command on September 4, 1882.[33]

One of Crook's first endeavors was to assemble Apache chiefs and headmen at San Carlos for a grand council. The meeting was convened on October 15, 1882, with some 400 Apache leaders present, and lasted until November 3. This was a preliminary step in trying to pacify any unrest among the reservation Apaches so that Crook could move forward against hostiles without fear of unexpected breakouts from the Indian agencies.[34]

At the same time, Crook came to his command with the assurance that he was free to act against hostiles fleeing to the sanctuary of Mexico. On July 29, 1882, Mexico and the United States government signed an agreement which permitted regular army troops of either country to cross the international border *if in close pursuit of hostile Indians.*[35] With that assurance, liberally interpreted by the general, as well as the neutrality of the reservation Apaches, Crook commenced in the late fall of 1882 to make his plans. Using Willcox, a station on the Southern Pacific Railroad in southeastern Arizona as a staging depot, "Forage, ammunition, and subsistence were brought in on every train . . . ."[36] But Crook still lacked two important ingredients in launching an overt offensive: he needed a guide who knew the Mexican terrain, and hopefully, the principal camp of the hostile Chiricahuas; secondly, an excuse to pursue hostiles across the border.

During the last ten days of March 1883, Crook got both ingredients. Beginning on March 21, hostile Chiricahuas from south of the border began murderous raids in the vicinity of Tombstone. Within a week, the hostiles killed at least 16 civilians. These deaths were capped by the slaying of Federal Judge and Mrs. H.C. McComas and the capture of their six-year-old son, Charlie, never to be heard of again.[37]

Again, scorned for its inability to stop the marauding bands, the Army took mounting public criticism in stride as it sent out cavalry units to try to intercept and destroy the roving hostile bands. On one such foray, Lieutenant Britton Davis's command, consisting of 30 scouts and a handful of Tonto Apache volunteers, captured Tso-ay, one of the roving hostiles, on March 31. Davis immediately took his prisoner back to San Carlos and wired the good news to Crook. In reply, Crook instructed the lieutenant to see if the prisoner could be enlisted as a guide and scout. A peace-loving Indian, Tso-ay's response was in the affirmative. He was immediately taken to Crook in Willcox. Thus, within less than a fortnight, Crook had a much needed guide in hand, who was quickly nicknamed "Peaches" by his army captors because he had a "light, pink, and smooth complexion."[38] He was the linchpin in Crook's final push to round up Geronimo in 1883. At the same time, the general also had his rational for hot pursuit because of the hostile incursions into southwestern Arizona. To further his plans, Crook went to Mexico to confer with the local authorities in order to pave the way for more cooperation and his planned offensive campaign. The trip was imminently successful.[39] All was now in place.

On May 1, 1883, Crook led his command south. It consisted of 193 scouts, commanded by Captain Emmet Crawford, assisted by Second Lieutenants Charles B. Gatewood and James O. Mackay. Al Sieber was Chief of Scouts, assisted by Archie McIntosh and Sam Bowman. Two interpreters were also in the command, Mickey Free and Severiano, both fluent in Spanish and Apache. No doubt Tom Horn was one of the army packers, although he would later claim a far more dominant role.

In addition, Captain Chaffee commanded a company of 6th Cavalry, 42

Brigadier General Orlando B. Willcox who succeeded Brigadier General George Crook after the latter's first tour of duty as commander of the Department of Arizona. *Courtesy National Archives, Washington, D.C.*

Apache scouts were one of the mainstays of army operations against hostiles and renegades during the Army/Apache conflict in Arizona and New Mexico territories. *Courtesy D'Arcy Indian Center, Newberry Library.*

TOM HORN'S SCOUTING DOMAIN
ARIZONA
VALENCIA
NEW MEXICO
SOCORRO
Prescott
Fort Verde
Fort Whipple
YAVAPAI
Chibicu Canyon
APACHE
Tonto Basin
White R.
White Mtns.
FORT APACHE RESERVATION
Fort Apache
MARICOPA
GILA
Verde River
Fort McDowell
Phoenix
Salt
River
Globe
San Carlos R.
Black River
Blue R.
SAN CARLOS RESERVATION
Ash Canyon
Clifton
River
Gila
River
Gila Valley
San Carlos
Fort Thomas
SOUTHERN PACIFIC RAILROAD
PINAL
GRAHAM
Ash Spring
Fort Bayard
Silver City
DOÑA ANA
Fort Grant
San Simon Valley
Stein's Peak
Doubtful Canyon
Mimbres R.
Tucson
PIMA
Dragon Mtns.
Fort Bowie
Chiricahua Mtns.
Deming
GRANT
UNITED STATES
Turkey Cr.
Whetstone Mtns.
Camp Rucker
MEXICO
UNITED STATES
MEXICO
Tombstone
COCHISE
San Luis Pass
Fort Huachuca
Skeleton Canyon
Cloverdale
Slaughter Ranch
San Bernardino
Sierra Media
Llano de Janos
N
Fronteras
San Luis River
Janos
River
Bavispe River
CHIHUAHUA
SONORA
Bavispe
Sierra Madre
Miles
0 25 50 75 100
0 25 50 75 100
Kilometer
Nacori
Aros River
Sonora
Yaqui River
River
Hermosillo

men in all. Others included two officers on Crook's staff, a surgeon, and a hospital steward. Accompanying the expedition's personnel was a pack train made up of various units, a total of 266 mules and 76 packers, half Mexican, half Anglo. As one historian rightly opines, "If Tom Horn accompanied the expedition, he did so as an ordinary packer."[40]

The expedition crossed the border at San Bernardino Ranch and commenced a 42-day march. The column struck southeast along the San Bernardino River, a northerly branch of the Yaqui. The trail progressively became more difficult, including the jungle of plants that made passage in the riverbed impossible. In short order, the Bavispe River was reached, followed by arrival at the towns of Bavispe, Bacerac, Hauchinera, and the ranch of Tesorababi where the column entered into the heart of the rugged Sierra Madre. Travel was grueling because of the formidable mountainous terrain. But press on the column did, daily progressing toward their target, the stronghold of the Chiricahuas.[41]

Captain Adna R. Chaffee who commanded at the Battle of Big Dry Wash Creek. He later rose to the rank of major general and retired to Los Angeles.

Peaches, one of Chatto's raiders, was recruited as a scout in Crook's last campaign against Geronimo. *Courtesy Arizona Historical Society.*

Sending a group of scouts ahead, on May 15 the enemy was encountered. Limited fighting ensued. The Chiricahuas had been found at last. In the days that followed, an increasing number of Indians, mostly women and children, came to the Americans' camp to surrender, gradually joined by reluctant braves. Finally, the crucial day arrived. On May 20, Geronimo came to parley with Crook. The next day he returned for further talk, eventually asking to be taken back to San Carlos with his followers. Meantime, other bands signaled their peaceful intentions by coming in to surrender. By May 28, a total of 374 Apaches, 123 warriors and 251 women and children had turned themselves in, including all the great leaders, with the exception of Juh. He and his family had defected from the Chiricahuas in the spring, striking out on his own, never to be heard of again.[42]

Mission accomplished, Crook headed north on May 30 for the return trip, shepherding some of the Apache along the trail. Other bands of Chiricahuas moved north, either independently or under escort. But it was

Brigadier General George Crook who served twice as commander of the Department of Arizona. In his first tour of duty he brought Geronimo to the San Carlos Reservation. On his second tour he was only partially successful in bringing the Chiricahua back to the reservation. *Courtesy Arizona Historical Society.*

General Crook with his staff and interpreters taken at Willcox, Arizona Territory, 1885. General Crook is the man with the white hat seated in the center. Tom Horn is the man with the white shirt who is kneeling third to the left of the general. To the right of the general, standing with the light, large brimmed hat, is Al Siebert. *Courtesy Arizona Historical Society.*

Brigadier Nelson A. Miles who succeeded Crook as commander of the Department of Arizona after Crook's second tour of duty and who obtained the final surrender of Geronimo. *Courtesy National Archives.*

not until February 1884 that the two principal leaders, Chatto and Geronimo, finally made their appearance at San Carlos, accompanied by their followers. For the time being, peace had been secured on the southwestern frontier.[43]

Horn's narrative of the Sierra Madre demonstrates that he certainly was a member of the expedition. Further than that, one must take a jaundiced view of what he records as fact. Indeed, one noted authority is blunt; he simply labels it "Horn's fictitous narrative."[44] There is much truth in that assertion.

What Horn tries to do is to play up the role that he and Sieber had in the negotiations with Geronimo on May 20 and 21, plus other items he inflates. In particular, Horn paints a grave picture of danger that Crook faced in his personal encounters with the Chiricahua leader, thus giving himself a starring role in those negotiations. Indeed, Horn makes himself almost a personal confidant of the general![45] One has to support the obvious conclusion that "the veracity of Tom Horn. . .most assuredly has been discredited abundantly."[46]

In detailing his last two years of service in the Army/Apache conflict in the Southwest, 1884-1886, Horn's autobiography has scrambled and inter-mingled events which took place in Crook's last year of commanding the Department of Arizona with that of his successor, Brigadier General Nelson A. Miles. In addition, he mistakenly has himself appointed Chief of Scouts to succeed Sieber in November 1884, which actually did not occur until November 1885. Yet, even with these patent discrepancies, his recounting of happenings between 1884 and 1886 does have information of import, much of it reliable.[47]

As for Horn, between November 1884 and the summer of 1885, he was on the go much of the time in pursuit of lingering renegade Apaches, mostly those who moved back and forth across the Arizona-Mexican border. By May 1885, the long-seething, pent-up resentment of the Chiricahuas against reservation life reached explosive proportions. The first major breakout occurred at Fort Apache on May 18, when Geronimo led some 50 adherents, under cover of darkness, to sanctuary in Mexico.[48] To counter this breakout, Crook dispatched two columns south into Mexico in early summer 1885: Captain Emmet Crawford, with Troop A, 6th Cavalry, 92 Indian scouts under Second Lieutenant Britton Davis, Al Sieber as Chief of Scouts, and Mickey Free as interpreter, accompanied by two pack trains, departing June 11; on July 13, the second column under Captain Wirt Davis, with Troop F, 4th Cavalry, 100 Indian scouts under

First Lieutenant Matthias W. Day, Charles B. Roberts and Frank Leslie, Chief of Scouts, plus two pack trains. Contrary to Horn's autobiography, he was not Chief of Scouts replacing an ailing Sieber; that is pure nonsense. Again, most likely, Horn went along with the Crawford contingent as one of the scouts under Britton Davis' command, having moved up the ladder from a lowly mule packer. But these expeditions failed to intercept or locate the Geronimo-led Apache renegades. While Davis continued to operate south of the border, Crawford returned to Arizona.[49]

As a result, it was decided to send a stronger second expeditionary force across the border. Again, Crawford was placed in command, but his contingent consisted solely of Indian scouts. When Sieber was summoned to serve as Chief of Scouts, he declined and suggested Horn. Thus, it was on November 29, 1885, when the Crawford column headed south, with Lieutenant Marion P. Maus as commander of the scouts, Horn went along as Chief of Scouts.[50] One historian rightly declared:

> Horn should be the best authority for this period [1885-1886], since he apparently was the only participant to publish a book about it. But his account is so hopelessly inaccurate and untrue as to be virtually worthless. For example, Horn, who has an excellent memory for some things, unaccountably confused Crook's and Miles's campaigns, lending weight to the theory that he did not write his "autobiography" bearing his name.[51]

The second Crawford command came close to success. On January 9, 1886, after weeks of demanding travel and hardship, it finally located the Geronimo-led Chiricahuas' camp. It was discovered south of the Aros (Haros) River, 60 miles south of the town of Nacori, and was occupied the next day. Most of the hostiles, however, escaped, but "their herd and camp outfit were taken."[52] Geronimo was not present at the time, even though Horn casts him in a dramatic role, urging his people to "break for the river."[53] But with horses, supplies, and equipment captured, Geronimo was in dire straits.

In the meantime, Mexican officials were becoming increasingly critical of the Army's Apache scouts, whom they alleged were committing depredations against Mexican nationals. Protesting directly to Crook, the general cautioned Crawford to be alert to any such untoward scout conduct.[54] This dispatch Crawford never received; he was mortally wounded on January 11.

On that date, a Mexican command, which included some Tarahumari scouts, mortal enemies of the Apache, also in search of Chiricahuas, came across the American camp. Immediately, "the camp was alarmed. . .by a

Captain Emmet Crawford who was mortally wounded in an encounter with Mexican troops while chasing Apache renegades. *Courtesy Arizona Historical Society*.

Apache scouts' camp. *Courtesy D'Arcy Indian Center, Newberry Library*.

Lieutenant Marion P. Maus who succeeded Captain Emmet Crawford on the latter's death while in pursuit of Apache renegades. *Courtesy Arizona Historical Foundation, Arizona State University, Tempe.*

shower of bullets." Crawford, Maus, and Horn tried in vain to halt the attack by waving handkerchiefs and yelling in Spanish. To no avail. The shooting continued for 15 minutes, when it abruptly ceased; it appears the Mexicans had realized their mistake. Lieutenant Maus best describes what happened next:

> A party of them then approached and Captain Crawford and I went out about fifty yards from our position in the open and talked to them. . .I told them in Spanish we were American soldiers, called attention to our dress and said we would not fire. . .Captain Crawford then ordered me to go back and ensure no more firing. I started back, when again a volley fired. . .When I turned again I saw the Captain lying on the rocks with a wound in his head, and some of his brains upon the rocks. This had all occurred in two minutes. He was said to be waving his handerkerchief when shot. Mr. Horn was also wounded at the same time in the left arm. . .*There can be no mistake; these men knew they were firing at American soldiers; at this time.* I took command. . . .[55]

In retaliation, the Americans returned the fire. In addition to Crawford's mortal wound (he died January 18) and Horn's lesser wound, two other Americans were wounded. The Mexicans had four dead and five wounded.[56]

The next day Maus entered into negotiations with the Mexicans, only to be threatened by them if he did not provide mules in compensation for their fatalities. Having complied with this request, to ease the tension he then moved his camp four miles farther on. It was there, on January 13, that he received two squaws on behalf of Geronimo who wished to council. To show his good faith, the Apache leader sent his own family and that of another leader, along with Nana, a feared chief in his own right, as a token of his serious intent to negotiate an agreement. Accompanied by 22 other warriors, who decided to accompany Maus back north, the American column headed for Arizona. By mid-March, only 75 of the hostiles had returned, but not the diehard Geronimo.[57]

Setting the rendezvous at the Canyon de los Embudos (Canyon of the Tricksters), Geronimo awaited the arrival of a small Crook-led delegation to open negotiations. It proved to be a difficult and trying meeting, one carried on from March 25-27. In the end, the negotiations proved successful. Geronimo agreed to return to San Carlos. With success in hand, Crook and his party returned north, while Lieutenant Maus was left with his contingent to escort the Indians back to the post. En route, Geronimo and a hard-core group of Chiricahuas bolted after consuming a quantity of mescal supplied by an American, who then proceeded to poison their minds against surrender. On the night of March 29, in a drizzling rain, the band stole away. This misadventure cost Crook his command. He was transferred to the Department of the Platte, effective April 28, and was succeeded in the Department of Arizona by Brigadier General Miles.[58]

Miles assumed command on April 12 upon reaching Fort Bowie.[59] After a conference with Crook, he settled in to his new post. One of the innovative things he did was to introduce the use of the heliograph. This was a device which, by the use of mirrors, could direct a beam of sun rays in any direction. Through the use of a shutter, messages could be sent by Morse code. Since the telegraph was easily cut by rampaging Indians, it was decided to adopt this method of communications for the Arizona-New Mexico theater.

When Miles arrived, he requested the best instruments and operators and, by August 1886, had an extensive network in place, comprised of 14 stations in Arizona and 13 in New Mexico. It helped play an important role in Geronimo's final renegade days. After his surrender, the system was dismantled.[60]

From a tactical point of view, Miles simply replaced Crook's use of Indian scout columns for operations south of the border with regular U.S. Army troops. He organized a cavalry command under Captain Henry W. Lawton and First Lieutenant Leonard Wood, both chosen for their outstanding physiques, to push across the border in search of the hostiles. The command consisted of one company of infantry, a troop of 35 handpicked cavalrymen, and 20 Indian scouts "with Tom Horn as Chief of Scouts," with 100 pack mules and 30 packers. It appears that Horn was with Lawton's command from the outset of its formation. Thus, the final great chase was launched in April 1886. Within five days in the rugged mountain terrain, the cavalry had to join the infantry afoot. For five grueling months, the column wearily searched for the Geronimo band, which probably numbered no more than two dozen or so Chiricahuas.[61]

In July, Miles learned that the renegades were negotiating the prospect of surrender to the Mexicans at Fronteras. He immediately dispatched Lieutenant Charles B. Gatewood south with the intelligence on July 13, accompanied by two Chiricahuas as guides. Gatewood reached Lawton's camp on the Aros River, some 250 miles south of the border, August 3, 1886. The company immediately proceeded northward, making for Fronteras in hopes of intercepting the Geronimo band.[62]

It was a swift and demanding march. Lawton sent Gatewood ahead on August 20, with 22 scouts, among them Tom Horn. Since the weather had turned rainy, travel was made more difficult. Finally, at long last, on

View of Fort Bowie, 1884, which was
the principal center of the army's
campaign against the Chiricahuas.
Courtesy Arizona Historical Society.

Lieutenant Charles B. Gatewood,
accompanied by Horn as scout and
translator, negotiated Geronimo's
final surrender. *Courtesy Arizona
Historical Society.*

Apache Indian police lined up in front of the guardhouse at the San Carlos Indian Reservation, Arizona Territory (A.T.) *Courtesy Arizona Historical Society.*

August 24, contact was made. Gatewood entered negotiations directly with Geronimo. He proved a wily and probing negotiator, asking direct and interesting questions. He was no dummy; that is for sure. Leaving the Indian to think over his response, Gatewood, accompanied by Horn, who acted as Apache interpreter, returned to his men for the night. The next morning Geronimo made his decision known: he would surrender and place his trust in General Miles, as Gatewood had urged.

Shortly after, Lawton and Wood reached the encampment. Gatewood explained to them, in detail, the negotiations and the outcome, much to their approbation. There is no doubt: Gatewood's handling of the negotiations led directly to the surrender of Geronimo and his followers. The credit is his.[63] The outstanding authority on the Army/Apache conflict in the Southwest has this praise for the role played by Tom Horn. He put it this way: "No writing I have seen gives Horn credit for the courageous, able work he did with the Lawton column; but he had the stuff of greatness, if lamentably, he had other less admirable qualities as well."[64]

On August 25, the Lawton column headed northward, escorting the surrendered Indians. Since Mexican forces were in the vicinity seeking revenge against the Chiricahuas, the force had to be vigilant. Sure enough, on August 28, some 180 Mexican soldiers were spied several miles distant. By dint of bluff and steadfastness, coupled with the Mexican soldiers' lack of organization, the threat evaporated. When the Mexicans were finally convinced that the Chiricahuas had surrendered, the Lawton column moved on without further intervention or encounters. Pushing forward to the appointed rendezvous, Skelton Canyon, where General Miles was to

42

council with Geronimo, there was a sense of growing uneasiness among the Indians. On one occasion, the prospect of a breakout was barely contained and Gatewood had his hands full trying to keep Geronimo in tow. A reluctant Miles finally appeared on September 3. The terms, which Gatewood had arranged, were confirmed by the general. Natchez, actually the chief of the band, and Geronimo accepted. The day after, Miles headed for Fort Bowie, taking with him in his ambulance the two leaders and a few others. They reached Bowie that same day, September 5. The rest of the party took three more days to reach the same post. En route, three men and women fled back to Mexico, the only defections.

The fate that befell the Chiricahuas and many other Apaches was exile to Florida. On September 8, Geronimo and his party boarded the train for the long trip east. The last holdouts, Mangus and his small band of men, women, and children, a dozen in all, surrendered in October. They, too, were sent to Fort Marion, Florida, to join their brethren in exile.[65] Thus ended the 23-year Army/Apache conflict in the Southwest. The wars were over, never to be resumed.

As for Tom Horn, his army days were also over. With the departure of Geronimo's party on September 8, Horn took his "scouts back to the [San Carlos] reservation, discharged them" and was himself discharged. He returned to the Aravaipa and began to work his mine, one he had long neglected. There he spent the winter of 1886-1887.[66] A chapter in his life

Fort Bowie as it appeared in 1885. Note the addition of several outbuildings. *Courtesy Arizona Historical Society.*

was thus completed. The first phase of his life at age 26 was over. A different and new way of life lay before him, one that, in the end, would lead to the gallows.

NOTES

1. Two biographies have centered on Horn's life. The best is Jay Monaghan, *Last of the Badmen: The Legend of Tom Horn* (Indianapolis and New York, 1946). Much less reliable is Lauran Paine, *Tom Horn, Man of the West* (Barre, Mass., 1963). I have relied on Monaghan for basic biographical details, pp. 14-55.
2. *Life of Tom Horn, Government Scout and Interpreter Written by Himself: A Vindication,* ed. by Doyce B. Nunis, Jr. (Chicago, 1987), p. 3. (Hereinafter cited *Life of Tom Horn.*)
3. *Ibid.,* pp. 12-16; Monaghan, *Last of the Bad Men,* pp. 30-35.
4. Monaghan, *Last of the Bad Men,* pp. 33-44.
5. *Ibid.,* pp. 42-44.
6. *Ibid.,* pp. 44-50.
7. *Life of Tom Horn,* p. 16.
8. *Ibid.,* p. 17.
9. *Ibid.,* pp. 17-18.
10. Dan L. Thrapp. *Al Sieber, Chief of Scouts* (Norman, 1964), for a comprehensive biography.
11. *Life of Tom Horn,* p. 21. Horn's chronology simply does not square even with his own writing for the period 1875-1882. He places himself in Santa Fe in December 1874 and declares he met Sieber at Camp Verde in July 1876. This is fully discounted by Monaghan in his biography, for Horn simply skips his activities from the summer of 1874 to the winter of 1877, which distorts his dates completely.
12. Sieber's letter is printed in full in the first edition of *Life of Tom Horn,* pp. 311-314.
13. *Life of Tom Horn,* pp. 25-41. At the end of his stay with Pedro's band, Horn relates that he then went prospecting and was present at the initial Tombstone discovery by Edward Schieffelin. *Ibid.,* pp 42-46. He then states he was summoned to return to Fort Whipple for army duty. This, without question, is another fabricated story.
14. *Ibid.,* pp. 64-65. Monaghan, *Last of the Bad Men,* p. 54, agrees with the *Life of Tom Horn* that he was employed by Tully, Ochoa & DeLong in July 1879. In structuring the Horn chronology, this would be a year off and should actually be July 1880 at best.
15. Dan L. Thrapp, *General Crook and the Sierra Madre Adventure* (Norman, 1972), pp. 128-129.
16. *Life of Tom Horn,* p. 46.
17. Thrapp, *Sieber,* pp. 220-221, 258.
18. *Life of Tom Horn,* pp. 64-67; John B. Harte, "The Strange Case of Joseph J. Tiffany," *Journal of Arizona History,* 16 (Winter 1975): 383-404, and John C. Bourke, *On the Border with Crook* (New York, 1891), pp. 438-440, presents the prevailing opinion of the time by quoting verbatim the grand jury report, as published in the Tucson *Arizona Star,* October 24, 1882, and giving it his approbation. Harte presents convincing detail that Tiffany was innocent of the charges and subsequent slander.
19. Typical of Horn, he places the fight at Cibicu Creek after his recounting of the Tupper-Loco fight, an ample demonstration of his confusion over chronology. A compact account is found in Cornelius C. Smith, "The Fight at Cibicu," *Arizona Highways,* 32 (May 1956): 2-5.
20. A first-hand account of the fight is found in Thomas Cruse, *Apache Days and After* (Caldwell, Idaho, 1941), pp. 102-112. For a good summary, see Dan L. Thrapp, *Conquest of Apacheria* (Norman, 1967), pp. 221-226.
21. Thrapp, *General Crook,* pp. 28-31, 36.
22. *Life of Tom Horn,* pp. 121-136.
23. William C. Barnes, "The Apaches' Last Stand in Arizona," *Arizona Historical Review,* 3 (January 1931): 58-59.
24. Thrapp, *General Crook,* p. 74-78.
25. Thrapp, *Conquest of Apacheria,* pp. 231-250, and *General Crook,* pp. 76-90, provide good summaries of the Loco flight and fight.
26. A first-hand account is provided in George A. Forsyth, *Thrilling Days in Army Life* (New York, 1900), pp. 79-120.
27. *Life of Tom Horn,* pp. 105-110; Thrapp, *Crook,* pp. 91-95.
28. Thrapp, *Conquest of Apacheria,* p. 254.

29. First-hand accounts are found in Cruse, *Apache Days and After,* pp. 158-176, and Britton Davis, *The Truth About Geronimo* (New Haven, 1929), pp. 11- 28. A good summary of operations is found in Thrapp, *Sieber,* pp. 244-257.

30. *Life of Tom Horn,* pp. 112-136, details his supposed role and view of Chevelon's Fork, sometimes called General's Spring Canyon, Canon Diablo, as well as Big Dry Fork or Big Dry Wash. The best guess is that the encounter took place on East Clear Creek, west of General's Spring Canyon.

31. *Ibid.,* pp. 139-141.

32. *Ibid.,* pp. 141-142.

33. Thrapp, *General Crook,* pp. 101-102.

34. Thrapp, *Conquest of Apacheria,* pp. 216-262.

35. *U.S. Statutes at Large,* XII:934.

36. John G. Bourke, *An Apache Campaign in the Sierra Madre* (New York, 1886), p. 28.

37. Thrapp, *Conquest of Apacheria,* pp. 267-270.

38. Bourke, *An Apache Campaign,* pp. 30-33; Davis, *Geronimo,* p. 57.

39. Thrapp, *General Crook,* pp. 123-125.

40. *Ibid.,* p. 128; Thrapp, *Conquest of Apacheria,* p. 300.

41. Thrapp, *General Crook,* pp. 131-137.

42. Thrapp, *Conquest of Apacheria,* pp. 286-291.

43. *Ibid.,* pp. 291-294, 303.

44. *Ibid.,* p. 300.

45. *Life of Tom Horn,* pp. 205-313, gives his fictitious version.

46. Thrapp, *Conquest of Apacheria,* p. 300.

47. *Life of Tom Horn,* pp. 243-316, covers this period.

48. Thrapp, *Conquest of Apacheria,* pp. 311-315.

49. *Ibid.,* pp. 328-335.

50. *Ibid.,* p. 339; Thrapp, *Sieber,* p. 313.

51. Thrapp, *Conquest of Apacheria,* p. 339, *note* 31.

52. *Ibid.,* p. 340.

53. *Life of Tom Horn,* pp. 261-265.

54. Thrapp, *Conquest of Apacheria,* pp. 340-341.

55. From Crook's *Annual Report,* Appendix K, January 21, 1886, as quoted in Thrapp, *Conquest of Apacheria,* p. 341. Maus' personal narrative is reprinted in *Personal Recollections and Observations of General Nelson A. Miles* (Chicago and New York, 1897), pp. 450-471. Also, see Bernard C. Nalty and Truman R. Strobridge, "Captain Emmet Crawford, Commander of Apache Scouts, 1882-1886," *Arizona and the West,* 6 (Spring 1964): 30-40.

56. Thrapp, *Conquest of Apacheria,* p. 342.

57. Angie Debo, *Geronimo: The Man, His Time, His Place* (Norman, 1976), pp. 250-253.

58. George F. Crook, *General George Crook: His Autobiography,* ed. by Martin F. Schmitt (Norman, 1946; rev. ed., 1960), pp. 260-261. A verbatim record of the negotiations is found in Davis, *Geronimo,* pp. 200-213.

59. Thrapp, *Conquest of Apacheria,* p. 350.

60. Henry P. Walker and Don Bufkin, *Historical Atlas of Arizona* (2nd ed., Norman, 1986), p. 27B; Bruno J. Polak, "General Miles' Mirrors: Heliography in the Geronimo Campaign of 1886," *Journal of Arizona History,* 16 (Summer 1975): 145-160.

61. Thrapp, *Conquest of Apacheria,* p. 352. Herman Hagedorn, *Leonard Wood, A Biography* (2 vols., reprint ed. of 1938; New York, 1969), I:75-103, gives a good account of the column's field sojourn, as does Thrapp.

62. Thrapp, *Conquest of Apacheria,* pp. 353-354.

63. Gatewood provides a detailed account of the negotiations in his article, "The Surrender of Geronimo," *Proceedings of the Annual Meeting and Dinner of the Order of Indian Wars of the United States* (Washington D.C., 1929), pp. 7-19, and in "Gatewood Reports to His Wife from Geronimo's Camp," ed. by Charles Byars, *Journal of Arizona History,* VII (Summer 1966): 76-81. Later Lawton tried to hog the credit, but history tells us otherwise. See R.G. Carter, "Lawton's Capture of Geronimo," *Collier's Weekly,* XXIV (January 27, 1900): 8. Thrapp, *Conquest of Apacheria,* pp. 354-360, offers a fine summary of the finding and surrender of Geronimo; he gives Gatewood full credit for same.

64. *Ibid.,* p. 352, *note* 9.

65. *Ibid.,* pp. 361-366. *Life of Tom Horn,* pp. 293-315, gives his detailed view of the chase, locating, and surrender of Geronimo.

66. *Life of Tom Horn,* p. 316.

From Cowboy to

2
Cattle Detective

orn's autobiography ends on an enigmatic note. He gives short shift to his post-Apache days, providing only the bones of an outline of his subsequent life. Before turning to an evaluation of his years in Arizona, the fleshing out of his life, until his dramatic death, would appear to be in order. As the reader will see, the circumstances surrounding his death have colored later perceptions of him.

With the exile of the hostile Apaches to Fort Marion, Florida, in September 1886 by General Miles, Horn's scouting days were soon ended. He filled his time with either employment as a cowhand for local ranchers or in mining modest claims near Tombstone. His first post-army job was in Arizona, punching cattle for the Chiricahua Cattle Company on the Mexican border. That employment was abruptly terminated when he was confronted by a Mexican lieutenant at a dance — the soldier's girl friend was apparently the cause — who drew on Tom, fired and missed. Horn's return fire did not. This reputedly was his first known killing (if one assumes the San Antonio shoot out years before, when he was a young greenhorn cowboy, did not result in a death from his gun).[1]

Drifting north from the border, Tom's immediate involvements remain obscure. It appears, however, that he traveled to the Tonto Basin and played a murky role in the Pleasant Valley War, the famed Graham-Tewksbury vendetta which violently erupted in February 1887. The two primary attributions for the cause of this bloody episode in Arizona history, the only one of its kind for that state in fact, are given as a classic confrontation between sheepmen and cattlemen, contesting for the range; the other is more prosaic–organized cattle rustling.[2] Horn sided with the latter, for in his autobiography he wrote: "Early in April, 1887, some of the boys came down from Pleasant Valley, where there was a big rustler war going on and the rustlers were getting the best of the game."[3]

Tom Horn in later life. *Courtesy Arizona Historical Society.*

Although the half-Indian Tewksbury boys had been good friends with the Iowa-born Graham brothers, that cordial relationship began to fray in 1883, turning into open violence four years later. Hired guns and organized gangs became contending forces, aided and abetted by the vengeful Grahams and Tewksburys and their respective neighboring allies. The wild mountain country north of Globe, centered in and around Pleasant Valley, became the battleground.

The Graham-Tewksbury Feud, better known as the Pleasant Valley War, broke out in 1887. The feud, sparked by rustling activity, was later inflamed when the Tewksburys drove sheep, owned by the Daggs brothers of Flagstaff, into the Tonto Basin of present-day Gila County. Most of the settlers in the area, who were cattlemen, joined the Grahams in forcefully opposing this move. The war lasted five years, and in the end the sheep were driven out. But the cost was very high: 29 men died, including every male Graham, with only Ed Tewksbury surviving from his family.

There are five versions of Horn's participation in the bloody struggle which ensued during the months of 1887-1888. The first is Horn's. He claims that he "was the mediator, and was deputy sheriff under Bucky O'Neill, of Yavapai County, under Commodore [Perry] Owens, of Apache County, and Glenn Reynolds, of Gila County." Horn's more reliable biographer concluded that he was retained by "neutral ranchmen in Pleasant Valley — thrifty and pacific husbandmen, chiefly Mormons — who wanted peace." However, he also hedges by noting that "Old-timers remember that he was intimate with the Tewksburys." A third view is that Horn was a hired gun (or rifle) for the Tewksburys in that conflict,which cost over two dozen lives. A personal friend recalled that John Rhodes, who was in charge of a cattle ranch in Pleasant Valley and for whom Tom had previously worked on a San Pedro River outfit, "sent for Horn to come and help him maintain an armed neutrality and protect his employer's interests. Together they kept clear of any connection with either faction." Besides, "Tom was then a deputy under the sheriffs of Gila and Yavapai counties." His mentor and friend, Al Sieber, concurs in this. He later wrote that Horn "went to work in Pleasant Valley as a ranch hand. After this, there was a fierce war in this section known as the Pleasant Valley War, between the cowmen and the sheep men ... Tom took no part with either side, although every inducement was offered him to take sides."[4] The weight of evidence here suggests that Horn played a neutral role (and that would embrace being a mediator) and was in the service of established law officials.[5]

In respect to the latter, as a deputy for Sheriff Bucky O'Neill of Yavapai County, Horn is reported to have killed five train robbers near Willcox and to have made numerous arrests of "many outlaws and bad Indians." As a result of this, he boasted about these killings which became a "stock in trade when he recounted these escapades. How many men, red and white, Tom killed in Arizona will never be known definitely."[6]

While engaged in deputy sheriff police work, which was a sometimes affair, Horn also accepted cowhand jobs and participated in riding and roping contests. The latter led to his setting a world record for roping and tying a steer in Phoenix at the territorial fair in 1891, besting his archrival, "Arizona Charlie" Meadows, a man whose life he had helped save from hostiles in 1882. His record, 49 and a half seconds, was the marvel of its day. No wonder "he had a choice of employment, being welcome at any ranch" in his post-army days. This reputation led to employment as foreman on the ranch of D.H. Ming and his partner, E.A. Jones, from October 1886-1888, followed by a similar ranch job with Burt Dunlop in Graham County, 1888 to May 1890. He also worked a few mining claims off and on. But more. When propositioned by Colonel William F. Cody to join "Buffalo Bill's Wild West Show and Congress of Rough Riders," Horn rejected the handsome, salaried offer outright, while Meadows accepted with alacrity. Horn preferred reality to artifice.[7]

A year before his world record mark, Horn met Cyrus W. Shores, better know as "Doc" Shores, the sheriff of Gunnison County, Colorado. There are two versions of how they met. One has it that Shores sent an inquiry to a local Pleasant Valley postmaster as to the whereabouts of two young men wanted for horse stealing and included a picture of one of the culprits. The postmaster immediately recognized the suspect, who worked on a nearby ranch in Box Canyon of the Aravaipa, and remembered that he had a partner working at Eureka Springs some 20 miles north. Sharing this intelligence with Horn, Tom responded by urging that the Gunnison sheriff be quickly informed. This was done. The postmaster went to Willcox, 60 miles distant, where Shores was at the time, "and gave him and Tom Horn his speedy road mules and buckboard to corral the two sought-after rustlers." At each of the two stops, Horn entered the ranch house to make the arrest while "Doc" Shores waited outside. The other version has "Doc" Shores coming to Arizona looking for a single culprit, a horse thief. Horn was recommended to Shores as a reliable man to assist in tracking and apprehending the thief. Their joint effort quickly proved successful. Both of these accounts, although varying in specific detail, conclude that

Shores' encounter with Horn had left an impression on the Colorado sheriff that the 30-year-old cowboy-lawman had the qualities necessary to make a good Pinkerton man. Shores, although elected sheriff in 1884 and served eight years in that capacity, occasionally worked on the side as an agent for the Pinkerton Detective Agency. Shores prevailed on Horn to return with him to Colorado. There he introduced his new friend to James McParland, head of the Denver-based office of the famed agency. As a result, in 1890, Horn became an operator for the firm.[8]

Horn's Pinkerton service is highlighted by his own account of tracking the McCoy train robbery gang with Shores which resulted in the speedy apprehension of gang members Burt Curtis and Thomas "Peg-Leg" Eskridge (alias Watson), and later young Joe McCoy, the ringleader.[9] These captures cemented Tom's reputation as an operator. A lesser-known story is one of the more traumatic incidents in Horn's career with Pinkerton.

Horn was sent on an assignment by McParland to locate and return a Jim McCabe to Denver, a man wanted for wrecking a train in order to rob and pilfer it. Setting out by rail for Salem, Oregon, the trail led him south to Truckee, California, then to Reno, Nevada. McCabe was known for being a tin-horn–"an itinerant gambler who could not afford a first-rate layout and shook dice in a tin cup or horn." Reno was a natural for him even in those days. Systematic searches of all local saloons came to naught. Daily, as required, Horn wrote of his activities to J.S. Mack, the alias for McParland, his boss.[10] Determined to get his man, on the evening of April 9, 1891, having posted his regular letter to his superior, Tom boarded a midnight westbound train in order to hunt down the line. Before the train pulled out, he was arrested by four local lawmen, handcuffed and taken to the Reno jail. The charge: masked robbery of the faro dealer at Al White's Palace Hotel of $800 in $20 gold pieces.[11] When two of the arresting lawmen offered him the chance to square things by a gift of money, Horn refused on the grounds he was innocent. The lawmen summarily booked him for robbery. The local newspaper hailed the robbery as "the most daring and successful ever perpetrated in Reno if not the State." The news report continued by noting:

> Thomas C. Hale, alias Horn, who was arrested on the express train as it was pulling out and on whose person $272.20 in coin was found, claims to be Pinkerton detective and undoubtely is, but there is reason to believe that he is the robber. He is known to have been bucking at the tiger [gambling] in the afternoon previous to the robbery. In one place he represented himself as a cowboy and in another place said he was

a gambler. The mask, which was made of black sateen, from the back of a vest, was found yesterday by the officers, and a pistol found in Hale's valise — a 38-calibre, 5-inch barrel, Smith & Wesson, nickle-plated — was identified as that which the robber had in his hand, when he took the money.

Since Tom could not post a $1,000 bond, he was remanded to jail to await indictment proceedings before the grand jury.[12]

The most damning bit of evidence, since all the rest was purely circumstantial, was Horn's pocket diary. It had recordings of all train times, conductors' and brakemens' names, along with the use of a cypher for various notations. The grand jury remanded him to trial, which finally commenced on July 14. Employing J.L. Wines and J.W. Dorsey as his defense attorneys, the prosecution was led by District Attorney T.V. Julien and the flamboyant ex-Congressman, William Woodburn. The week-long trial ended in a hung jury, six for acquittal, six for conviction. Horn was summarily remanded over for retrial on motion by the district attorney.[13]

While awaiting his second trial, Horn was at liberty on bail, a bond no doubt made possible by the Pinkerton agency. It was not until September 29 that the retrial commenced. The prosecution team remained the same, Julien and Woodburn. But the defense was greatly augmented, apparently reflecting support from the agency. Tom's lawyers now included "Messrs. Baker, Wines & Dorsey and Benj. Curler." From the outset, the retrial proved highly contentious, signaled by the bitter challenges posed by both prosecution and defense to prospective jurors. It took much of the first day to empanel the jury. Formal court proceedings did not commence until 3:00 P.M., followed by adjournment to 7:00 P.M. that night.[14]

The State of Nevada vs. Thomas H. Horn offered the prosecution a grand opportunity to posture for the local audience, especially politician William Woodburn. But the spirited defense team carried the day. In doing so, the defense anchored their arguments on the character and established reputation of Horn. As the Reno newspaper reported:

> The first evidence introduced by the defense was in the form of depositions which had been taken in Arizona and New Mexico, where Horn formerly lived. Among the depositions was that of General Nelson A. Miles, which was a high testimonial of his honesty, efficiency and bravery while connected with the Indian service in Arizona. The other depositions were from prominent men in Arizona, ex-Sheriffs, U.S. Marshalls [sic] and Judges. All tended to the same point, and were to the effect that Horn was always well and favorably known as an honest and upright citizen, upon whom there had never been attached the slightest suspicion in any way.

To reinforce these depositions, two army officers, who had known Horn in Arizona, personally testified. The first, Lieutenant John M. Neall, then stationed at the state university, recalled knowing Horn from the time he was posted to duty at Fort Bowie. He declared that Horn "was a chief of scouts under his command; that he knew his general reputation and had a personal acquaintance with him; that his reputation was good and that he never heard anything derogatory to him." Neall was followed by Colonel Mason M. Maxon (incorrectly given in the report as Maxson) who "testified that he lived in Arizona in the early '80[s], and knew Horn and knew his reputation to be good."[15]

The clinching witness was no less than William A. Pinkerton, "Superintendent of Pinkerton's National Detective Agency." He told the court:

> . . . I know the defendant and he has been in my employ several years. He was sent to Salem, Oregon, to locate a man who is supposed to be connected with the Lake Labish disaster [staged train wreck], in the interest of the Southern Pacific Company. He was looking for a man by the name of McCabe. Horn was employed by me upon the credentials which he had. He has been a trusted employee of ours and while in our employ has been an honest and efficient employee.

To close the defense case, Horn was placed on the stand. He outlined the highlights of his life in Arizona where he "worked on ranches and broke horses," as well as being a ranch foreman and serving with the government "as an interpreter and scout and finally chief of scouts." He subsequently "worked for the Chiracahua Cattle Company, Ming & Jones, Bert Dunlop and at the San Carlos reservation for the Government." He related his service under Generals Crook and Miles "in the Apache war and was present at the time of and assisted in the capture of Geronimo. I had charge of 100 scouts," he declared.

Horn then moved on to his hunt for the suspect McCabe, noting that he went to Salem, Oregon, reaching there on December 3, 1890. He remained there until April 4, 1891, when he received instruction from the Denver office to go to Truckee where McCabe was supposed to be, only to draw a blank; then on to Reno. In way of illustrating his detective methods, he recalled that while in Salem, "in order to get in with the man I was hunting, I commenced work by day on a swamp ditch and worked right along with the men in order to gain their confidence. They were all ex-convicts. I slept with them and ate with them."

He then related his arrival and activities in Reno for the several days preceding his arrest. As he told it, "The evening of the robbery I was around town, playing at the games and visiting the saloons. I went down to Chase's to see if I could find the man McCabe." Then, he returned to his room in the Palace Hotel to write his daily report to Denver and went to mail it. (The postmaster concurred on the postmark which was the evening of April 9.) Hearing the train whistle below, he decided to catch it and proceed west along the line looking for McCabe. On boarding the train, he was summarily arrested. At that time, he told his arrestors,". . . I had no money but my own and had not committed any crime and had nothing to say." Prosecutor Woodburn could not shake Horn's testimony, even though he tried in every way.

The defense, apparently confident of the outcome, elected not to present a summation. Instead, the legal team "expressed a willingness to submit it without argument, to which the State finally assented." The four-day trial ended swiftly on October 2 after the judge's charge to the jury. "In a few minutes the jury found a verdict of 'not guilty,' and Thomas H. Horn was discharged and his bondsmen released."[16]

Horn's acquittal did not eradicate the bitterness he felt for his jailing and encounter with the law. The Reno episode undoubtedly left a deep psychological scar on his consciousness: his pride had been sorely wounded. Fortunately, the high opinion he was held in by the Pinkerton agency, and the staunch support rendered by his friend "Doc" Shores, insured Tom's return to the detective firm's good graces and continued employment.

In the ensuing two years, the humdrum of Pinkerton duty gradually began to wear thin on Horn. As he later explained, "my work for them was not the kind that exactly suited my dispostion; too tame for me."[17] It was little wonder that he terminated his association with the agency in 1894, seeking more unfettered and unrestricted employment on the open range as a Wyoming stock detective. But before describing this last phase in Horn's career, one matter must be dealt with categorically in order to set the record straight.

Jay Monaghan, who has authored by far the most reliable biography of Horn, as indicated previously, suggests in his book that Tom may have played a subtle, active role in the famed 1892 Johnson County War in Wyoming.[18] That cattle war pitted Wyoming cattle "kings" — more frequently called cattle barons — against the small ranchers. Indeed, the cattle barons, because of the vast size of their ranching operations, were easy prey to one-time cowboys turned homesteaders who knew how to use the lariat and branding iron illegally, to augment their small, fledgling herds. Because many of the barons were in the main absentee owners, easy going local law enforcement officials tended to side with the small ranchers, more numerous in number, thus more decisive at the polls. In the bargain, justice usually sided against the barons since jury trials were staffed by local veniremen. The barons' recourse was to form the Wyoming Stock Growers' Association (the more accurate title would be the Wyoming Cattlemen's Protective Association), and hire private stock detectives to root out and punish rustlers. Over a period of time, Johnson County, some 250 miles northwest of Cheyenne, became known for having the greatest concentration of cattle thieves among its ranching homesteaders. In a concerted effort to eradicate that situation, the association mounted and sent a vigilante force of 46 men to Johnson County to set matters right. Sometimes called the Invaders or Regulators, it included 19 cattlemen, 22 hired guns, and five stock detectives.

Departing Cheyenne on a special Union Pacific train in the late afternoon of April 5, 1892, under the leadership of Frank Wolcott and Frank H. Canton, three passenger cars carried the men and three baggage cars their horses. The company left the train at Casper, a 100 miles distant from their objective. In order to maintain the advantage of surprise, they cut the telegraph lines. But secrecy was not to be maintained. The local populace, alerted to the prospect before them, rallied and formed a sheriff's posse, some 200 strong. Thirteen miles south of Buffalo the posse surrounded the Invaders who had sought refuge in the TA Ranch house situated on Crazy Woman Creek. On receiving intelligence of what was transpiring and because he was a friend of the cattlemen's association members, the state's acting governor sought federal intervention by the U.S. Army. President William H. Harrison approved, and cavalry troops from Fort McKinney arrived in time to relieve the besieged Invaders and escort them safely to Cheyenne. There they were finally brought to trial in January 1893, skillfully defended by Willis Van Devanter, later an associate justice on the U.S. Supreme Court. He won an outright dismissal of the case due to the mysterious disappearance of two critical witnesses, and the fact that Johnson County did not have the revenue resources to finance the prosecution.[19]

In respect to Tom Horn, the Johnson County War has a very direct bearing on his last years and death. However, there is *no evidence* that he played a role, directly or indirectly, in recruiting gunmen from Texas to join the Invaders, as suggested by his biographer. Indeed, Monaghan qualifies this charge by noting that Horn's "enemies, knowing that his work with Pinkerton's led him up and down the Union Pacific," ardently

A special train on the Union Pacific in Wyoming, carrying private stock detectives of the Wyoming Cattlemen's Protective Association trying to root out and punish rustlers. *Donald Duke Collection.*

believed that he had recruited some of the hired guns, if not all, while Tom's friends staunchly held to the contrary.[20] What, in essence, the Johnson County War did was insure that the big cattlemen had only one recourse: to employ stock detectives to protect their herds from rustlers and to impose extra-legal range justice on cattle thieves. This became Horn's final calling; he became a stock detective.

A second impact on Horn, which emanated from the Johnson County War, was the long lingering hatred and bitter jealousy sown between the small ranchers and the cattle barons. That deep-seated enmity was literally institutionalized as a pervasive force in Wyoming's economic life and politics in the decade and half that followed.[21] It was into this milieu that Tom Horn came in 1894, making his debut in Wyoming as a private stock detective for hire.

Tom's first employer was octogenarian John Clay, a Scotsman, who was president of the Wyoming Stock Growers' Association. Clay, who had been in Scotland during the Johnson County War, was determined to protect his vast holdings in the valley of the Chugwater north of Cheyenne. To camouflage his real intent, Clay employed Horn ostensibly for his Swan Land & Cattle Company, a Scottish-based syndicate, to break horses, a job Tom could easily handle, as well as sleuthing for known rustlers.[22] In

56

no time at all, Horn's reputation for the latter was well established, so much so that "word of his presence in an area was sufficient to scare off many cattle and horse thieves."[23]

His next employer was the Wyoming Stock Growers' Association. However, since all of their range detective activities were highly confidential and top secret, one is left to surmise as to the extent of time and service rendered by Horn. One authority holds that J.M. Carey, who was the chairman of the association's secret committee charged with detective work, "is said to have dismissed Horn as soon as he learned that he was more interested in liquidating men than in getting evidence for use in court." After that dismissal, Tom free-lanced for some of the big cattlemen who "hired him to assassinate their enemies at five hundred dollars per head."[24]

Horn's methods were singular. Once a name of a troublemaker, be it either a suspected rustler or troublesome homesteader, was turned into him, he would set to work to locate the individual. Range justice was usually executed from ambush, his weapon, a high-powered rifle. Having meted out the punishment, Horn would then carefully remove any incriminating evidence, including shell casings, "set two stones under the head of his victim as a sort of trademark," and quietly leave the scene. For each of his executions, Tom received $600 in cash.[25] He reputedly boasted, "Killing is my specialty; I look at it as a business proposition, and I think I have a corner on the market."[26] But there was a major problem he had to deal with on leaving the employ of Swan Land & Cattle Company to strike out on his own as an independent — securing jobs. As his biographer aptly remarked: "Looking for work was irksome to his ego."[27]

With the advent of the Spanish American War, Horn found temporary respite from range sleuthing. But the idea of serving his country in uniform did not appeal to him. He knew the soldier's life from his Apache days and had long eschewed it as too confining, let alone his distaste for military discipline. An alternate form of service, more attractive to his life-style, was in the offing. The Army was sorely in need of experienced mule packers and handlers. Having learned from experience in the closing months of the Apache campaign, army planners realized that mule pack trains would be essential to all field operations in Cuba, Puerto Rico, and the Philippine Islands. So the word went out for civilian muleteers to sign on for contract service. Horn got wind of this development and headed for St. Louis where a large pack train was to be organized.[28] The Army planned each pack train to be headed by a "a chief packer, two pack masters,

20 packers, a 100 mules and a bell mare." When Tom enrolled, he entered service as a lowly packer. He should have made known his ability to speak Spanish. By the time his pack-mule outfit reached Tampa, Florida, bound for Cuba with Teddy Roosevelt's Rough Riders, he was one of 16 pack masters posted to that theatre of operations. It was at that embarkation, while Horn's outfit awaited transport, that he supposedly first met General William R. Shafter, the commanding general.

Finally, the appointed sailing date came. The transport ship set sail, reaching the beach at Daiquiri on June 22, the objective being the capture of Santiago. There the mules had to swim ashore, giving Horn plenty to do rounding them up. In a very short time, he ran across old friends from his Arizona days: first, Henry W. Lawton, now a major general; Sheriff Bucky O'Neill, a captain; Leonard Wood, a colonel; William E. Shipp, still a first lieutenant in the 10th Cavalry.

The campaign for Santiago was over in three short weeks. The city surrendered on July 17. But not without considerable cost. Twenty-three officers and 250 men gave their lives in the endeavor. The worst was yet to come: yellow fever and dysentery would take an equally heavy toll. When the final casualty figures were posted, one percent of the soldiers placed under arms during the Spanish American War in the Cuban theatre died: 113 officers, 2,803 men, 90 percent of them, victims of diseases.

On August 1, 1898, Tom was promoted to the rank of chief packer, placing him in charge of eight pack trains, at the modest salary of $133 a month and board. However, that service was short-lived. Fever laid him low. He was hospitalized and then evacuated to the mainland. On disembarking at New York, he turned to the Pinkerton office for aid in assisting him to return to Wyoming. Spanish American War veterans did not merit post-discharge assistance, least of all civilian contractees. With fare in hand, Tom boarded a train for Wyoming, where, once again, he found himself among friends who saw to it that he was nursed back to health.[29]

His health restored, Horn resumed his stock detecting as an independent, augmented by cowboy odd jobs. He reputedly took on assignments for a big rancher, Ora Haley, and made a number of forays into Colorado in pursuit of culprits. However, that employment is based on hearsay. By 1900, if not 1899, he was in the employ of John C. Coble, working for him on his Iron Mountain Ranch Company at Bosler, Wyoming. The two men quickly became close friends, indeed, confidants as attested to by Horn's letters to his employer. Coble, aristocratic and well-educated, but a die-hard cowman at heart, early on expanded his cattle ranching activities to

Horn was stock detecting for John C. Coble
at his Mountain Ranch Company at Bosler,
Wyoming, circa 1899-1900. *American
Heritage Center*

include horse ranching, locating his spread north of Laramie in the Iron
Mountain region of the Laramie range. Rumor had it that Coble and his
next-door neighbor and partner, Frank Bosler, looked to Horn to protect
their herds and property.[30]

Toward the end of 1900, the Iron Mountain School District employed a
Missouri schoolteacher, Glendolene Myrtle Kimmell. She came to Wyoming
in January 1901 and commenced teaching there in early July.[31] Whether he
recognized it or not, for Horn was not given to overt fraternization with
ladies, Miss Kimmell gradually developed a deep attachment to the tall
and aloof Horn. Destined to be his albatross, she, nevertheless, proved
steadfast to him to the end and beyond. But her attachment did him more
harm than good.

The occasion that led to Tom Horn's demise is shrouded in contradictions.
Probably no one will ever know the true facts. What is known is that on
the early morning of July 19, 1901, William Nickell, called Willie by his
family, the 14-year-old son of Kels P. Nickell, a local rancher, was dry-
gulched from ambush. Large for his age, Willie was riding his father's
horse and wearing his hat and yellow slicker when he was struck down by
two bullets in the early light of dawn. Were those bullets meant for his
father?

Willie Nickell, the 14-year-old who was reputedly gunned down by Tom Horn. *Courtesy American Heritage Center.*

The scene where Willie Nickell was killed. No. 1 - The rocks where the assassin hid. No. 2 - The gate where Willie was shot. No. 3 - Where Willie's body was found. *Courtesy American Heritage Center.* (Copyright 1902 by W.G. Walker, Cheyenne, Wyoming. Copyright renewed April 1953.)

Evidence points to the fact that Kels Nickell for over a decade had a running feud with his neighbor, James E. Miller. Both Nickell and Miller shared a strong dislike for John Coble after he moved into the area. Indeed, on one occasion, in an argument, Nickell pulled a knife and slit Coble's clothing down the front, leaving him with two bleeding, gashing wounds across his abdomen. In retaliation, Coble had Kels arrested. Pleading self-defense, he got off — a typical example of how justice was meted out when big cattlemen and small ranchers were involved. Later, Miller tangled with Nickell, knifing him in February 1901. The wound was serious, but he recovered. The Miller-Nickell feud culminated in a confrontation between the fathers and two of their respective sons, Miller urging his 17-year-old, Vic, to bash young Willie's head with a rock, only to miss. Now, Willie was dead, shot by an unknown assassin.[32]

These facts suggest several scenarios. First, was Willie's death attributable to the Miller-Nickell feud? Was the assassin gunning for Kels Nickell and mistakenly bushwhacked his young son? Or was this a case of a big cattleman taking range-justice action against a small rancher, who, only a few months before, had turned his back on cattle raising and brought sheep into the district — "an unpardonable sin in cattle country?"[33]

How does Tom Horn fit into these scenarios? Circumstantially at best. He was in the vicinity of the Nickells place on July 17-18. It was on July 17, in the evening, that he paid his first visit to the Miller ranch, having previously met Jim Miller who had extended him hospitality should Tom ever venture into his immediate neighborhood. Thus, this was Horn's first acquaintance with the Miller family. Nor did he know the Nickell's family, though he did know "Old Nick," the father. It was on that first and only visit, by invitation, to the Miller place that he met Miss Kimmell for the first time. She was a boarder there, having only assumed her teaching duties two weeks before at the Miller-Nickell school. From that evidence, it is clear that Tom only had hearsay about the Miller-Nickell feud and, thus, can not be accused of being a partisan of either party. However, he came into the area to check and see if Nickell's sheep had wandered onto the Coble range. Finding that such was not the case, he left the region on the day before young Willie was killed.[34] If this scenario is correct, then suspicion falls heavily on the Millers.

Miss Kimmell detailed this prospect in a lengthy statement that was published in the 1904 edition of Horn's autobiography. She noted that when young Nickell was found dead, three-quarters of a mile from his home, there were no clues. At the outset, "the Millers were immediately suspect."

> One theory was that Jim Miller, lying in wait for "Old Nick," as he called his arch-
> enemy, had shot the boy by mistake; but at the first session of the coroner's inquest,
> July 22nd, strong evidence tended to show that Victor Miller was the guilty one,
> having had many personal quarrels and fights with William Nickell. But the
> evidence was not strong enough to warrant an arrest, and it looked as though this
> tragedy would also remain unsolved.[35]

However, on August 3, Nickell's sheep wandered on to Miller's land. "Several hundred sheep taken from their owner's homestead, driven across the public range and down into a meadow of a neighbor's deeded land, was certainly provocation from a cattleman's standpoint." The quick withdrawal of the sheep narrowly averted bloodshed. But, the very next day the elder Nickell was shot and badly wounded: a shattered left arm near the elbow, a ragged hole in his left hip, and a minor wound under the right arm. He was immediately taken to Cheyenne for hospitalization. That same afternoon four masked men frightened off the sheepherder and clubbed 75 sheep to death. Though Miller and his sons, Gus and Vic, were later arrested on suspicion, their alibis held, and they were released without being charged.[36]

On August 9, the second session of the coroner's inquest was held. The younger Nickell children "testified that they had seen the men ride away" after the shooting of their father, "in the direction of the Millers', one on a bay and the other on a gray horse." This was damning evidence for Miller owned two such horses. The seriousness of the attempt against Nickell's life was underscored by the fact that 13 shots had been fired at him, three hitting the target.[37]

As Miss Kimmell tells it, the attempt on his life, compounded by the slaughter of his sheep, was the last straw for Nickell. He sent for his family to join him in Cheyenne, and then put "his ranch up for sale. The remainder of the flock was withdrawn from the country by their owners, Nickell having simply pastured the sheep on shares." As for Nickell, after his recovery, he went to work for the Union Pacific in October and disappeared into the mist of history.[38]

An interesting aspect to the suspicion that fell on the Millers was that Nickell and his wife told a neighbor: " 'They will try to lay this on Tom Horn, but he never done it! It was the Millers'.' " On the other hand, two of Miller's sons, Victor and August (Vic and Gus), "repeatedly said to [Miss Kimmell]: 'It's all right to let suspicion fall on Tom Horn! He doesn't care, and it might help us.' " And so it did, almost from the outset.[39]

Joseph LeFors, the U.S. Deputy Marshall for Laramie County, who undertook the investigation of Horn's case and solicited Horn's so-called confession. *Courtesy American Heritage Center.*

With the August 4 Nickell shooting and sheep killing, Sheriff Shafter, who suddenly became quite ill, critically so, asked Deputy United States Marshal Joseph LeFors to enter the case. A seasoned lawman, an excellent sleuth with long experience, LeFors eagerly accepted the invitation. Without public notice or fanfare, he began quietly working undercover to see if he could unravel the Nickell's homicide, and hopefully, other similar homicides perpetrated in the region.[40]

In the interim, between his departure from the Miller ranch on July 18 until September 1, Horn's activities were to become a matter of controversy, central to his defense when brought to trial. However, from September 1 and after, his presence is fairly well recorded for on that date he participated in the annual Frontier Days in Cheyenne, "with his famous bronco busters and fancy cattle ropers easily won first honors in the riding and roping contests." In the ensuing fall, he worked for Coble's Iron Mountain Ranch Company with a side excursion to Denver to take a load of horses to market for a local stockman. While in Denver, Tom became engaged in a drunken brawl in a saloon which resulted in a broken jaw that required three-weeks hospitalization.[41] That episode was to play a prominent part in Horn's subsequent defense.

During this same time interval, August to December, LeFors was busy at his undercover task of sleuthing the Nickell's crime. Gradually, his suspicion fell on Horn as a body of circumstantial evidence pointed in his direction, or so he later maintained. By happenstance, the two met, an introduction being solicited by the marshal. Their first meeting took place in a Cheyenne saddle shop where Horn was engaged in purchasing a gun scabbard and ordering one to be made for his 30-30 Winchester. As LeFors tells it: "We had quite a visit and talk about the Winchester, the sights, etc., the muzzle, velocity, penetration, etc., and I found Horn very well posted on small arms and *rather inclined to brag.*"[42] The latter was the characteristic LeFors spotted as Horn's Achilles heel; it was to be Tom's undoing. About the same time, the marshal established almost daily contact with Walter Stoll, the prosecuting attorney for Laramie County, who provided him a stenographer for ready dictation of any evidence discovered or uncovered.

LeFors first break was a casual encounter on a train where he struck up a conversation with a Bosler ranch boss known only as "George." In bringing up the Willie Nickell's case, LeFors set his trap. He called attention to the fact that three Pinkerton men were around Cheyenne watching Horn (which appears questionable in fact). Then the marshal sprung his trap: "Tom was drinking and I understood, talking about the Nickell case. Why don't you send him out of the country? Horn is going to get someone in trouble yet by his talk."

The implied bait here was obvious: Tom Horn knew the names of the cattlemen who had hired his stock detective services and might well betray one and all in a drunken stupor. The Bosler cattlemen would have to silence him, "they would have to bump him off themselves." Triumphantly, the marshal had found his first sure lead. As he writes, "This was my first real information that I could rely on — that Tom Horn was guilty of killing little Willie Nickell." The clincher for LeFors was the conversant's admission that "he did pay Horn for jobs committed before; that he paid Horn on the train between Cheyenne and Denver. The money . . . he paid him was in gold and paper money."[43]

LeFors set a second trap for a married lady who was sexually liberated, conduct which accorded her anonymity in the sources, for she was never called to testify. In the bargain, the lady had a penchant for "high-balls." Through enticement, coupled with liberal libations, she became talkative. The mystery lady gave a history of her adventures and then told the marshal, who was accompanied by a woman detective (again unnamed), how "she had carried sandwiches to Horn while he was lying in hiding to get a shot at Nickell, the father of Willie Nickell." She was sent home, her conversation was passed on to the prosecuting attorney.

Encountering the lady in question the next day, LeFors records that she told him bluntly, concerning Horn's involvement, " 'I did not know it at the time but I do suspect now.' " There was no witness to this second conversation, but the marshal rather ungallantly concludes: "The woman was just about as dangerous as Horn himself. I think she was about one-half Spanish or something, not entirely All-American."[44]

Now, thoroughly convinced of Horn's guilt, LeFors set his final trap, a trap for Horn himself. Knowing that the fall roundup season was over, he chose as his bait the prospect of a stock detective job in Montana and proceeded to arrange an offer for Tom from W.D. Smith, a well-known cattleman in Miles City. The offer was for $125 a month. Smith wanted "a good man to do some secret work . . . a man I can trust." The objective was to eradicate a nuisance rustler band. To insure the prospect that Horn would accept, LeFors contacted "George," the unnamed cattleman, who wanted Horn out of the country, and asked him to pressure Coble so that if Horn refused, "they would make him take it whether he wanted it or not."

LeFors' strategy paid off. Coble came to Cheyenne to talk over the Montana job offer with him, then asked to take the Smith letter back to Bosler to show it to Horn. This he did, and on January 1, 1902, Tom wrote LeFors a "Dear Joe" letter, which indicates a growing intimacy, if not friendship, on his part. He accepted Smith's offer, commenting, "I can guarantee him the recommendation of every cow man in the State of Wyoming in this line of work." Horn then boasted: "You can write Mr. Smith for me that I can handle his work and do it with less expense in the shape of lawyer & witness fees than any man in the business." Concluding, Horn wrote: "Joe, you yourself know what my reputation is although we have never been out together." The bait had worked; the trap was sprung.

A few days later, under cover of January 7, an exultant LeFors received a second Horn letter, "the letter I wanted," said he. A grateful Horn again boasted: "I will get the men sure, for I have never yet let a cow thief get away from me unless he just got up and jumped clean out of the country." He was ready to leave in ten days. The final lure was a train pass to Montana to be picked up from the marshal.[45]

The spider had spun its web well. Now, the finishing touch: entrapment. In anticipation of Horn's calling on him in Cheyenne before departing for Montana, LeFors prepared for the final denouement. He "put everything in readiness and planned to have the U.S. Court reporter and the deputy sheriff hide behind the door in the Clerk's office and take down a conversation between Tom Horn and me," which he carefully arranged. Such was the ultimate strategy to procure a "confession." To insure success, the marshal had a key maker "fix the door between the Clerk's and Marshal's office so that it could be locked and had him give it plenty of clearance so it would not drag." The end result was "about two inches of clearance under the partition door between the two offices."

When Horn reached Cheyenne on Sunday, January 12, he was met at the train by LeFors. Pointedly, the marshal later wrote in his memoirs: "I know that he was not drunk, as has been so often claimed," a crucial point of contention in the trial of Tom Horn to follow. The two went to the marshal's office. Behind the door, as prearranged, were Deputy Sheriff Leslie Snow and U.S. Court Reporter Charles Ohnhaus, acting as witness and stenographer, respectively. The dialogue that ensued between the two men became the heart of the case against Tom Horn for the killing of Willie Nickell. The conversation that was taken down by the listening court reporter appeared to be an outright confession. The essence was as follows:

> LeFors: What kind of gun have you got?
> Horn: I use a 30-30 Winchester.
> LeFors: Tom, do you think that will hold up as well as a 30-40?
> Horn: No, but I like to get close to my man. The closer the better.
> LeFors: How far was Willie Nickell killed?
> Horn: About 300 yards. It was the best shot I ever made, and the dirtiest trick I ever done. I thought at one time he would get away.

Then in a final reference to that homicide, LeFors asked Horn why he "killed the kid. Was it a mistake?" Horn replied, "Well, I will tell you all about it when I come back from Montana. It is too new yet."

Toward the end of this recorded conversation, Horn could not restrain his boasting nature, commenting: "I am 44 years, 3 months, and 27 days old, and if I get killed now I have the satisfaction of knowing I have lived about 15 ordinary lives." Then he continued, "I would like to have somebody who saw my past and could picture it to the public. It would be the most _______ _______ interesting reading in the country; and if we could describe to the author our feelings at different times it would be better still. The experience of my life, or the first man I killed, was when I was only 26 years old."

LeFors seized on this obvious display of bravura and pressed Horn on two other killings attributed to him. Cleverly, LeFors posed a question about the killings and then offered an answer: "How much did you get for

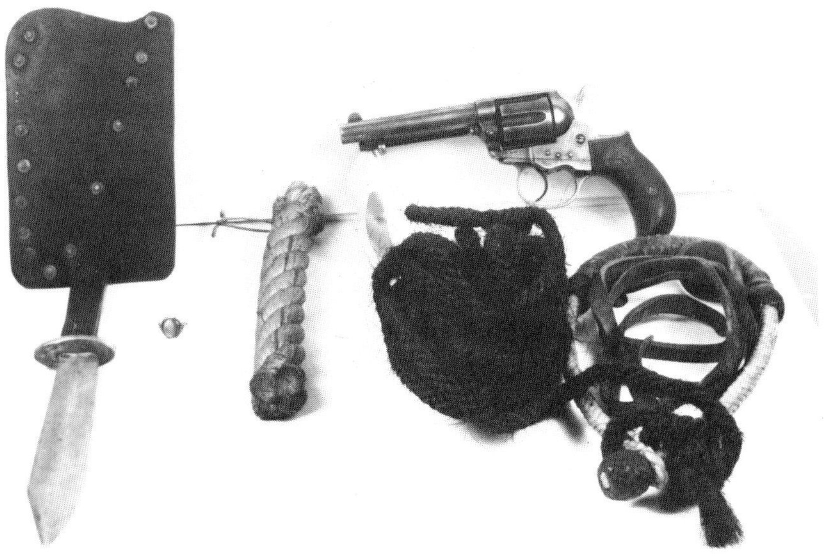

Tom Horn's personal weapons which were confiscated when he was placed under arrest for the murder of Willie Nickell. *Courtesy American Heritage Center.*

killing these fellows? In . . . [this] case you got $600 apiece." Horn, taken aback, asked LeFors, "How did you come to know that, Joe?"

LeFors cooly replied, "I have known everything you have done, Tom, for a great many years. I know where you were paid the money on the train between Cheyenne and Denver. Why did you put the rock under the kid's head after you killed him? That is one of your marks, isn't it?"

"Yes," Horn answered, "that is the way I hang out my sign to collect my money for a job of this kind."

Then, the final nail was driven into Horn's glaring confession. LeFors asked, "Have you got your money yet for the killing of Nickell?" To which Horn responded: "I got that before I did the job."

Intent on leaving no loose ends, LeFors slyly commented, "You got $500 for that. Why did you cut the price?" Horn calmly replied, "I got $2,100." Quick clarification made it clear that this included "three dead men and one man shot at five times." Then in a final burst of braggadocio, Horn triumphantly declared: "Killing is my specialty. I look at it as a business propostion, and I think I have a corner on the market."

The two men then "exchanged some stories" and adjourned to a nearby saloon for a drink. In the meantime, the stenographer hurriedly worked at

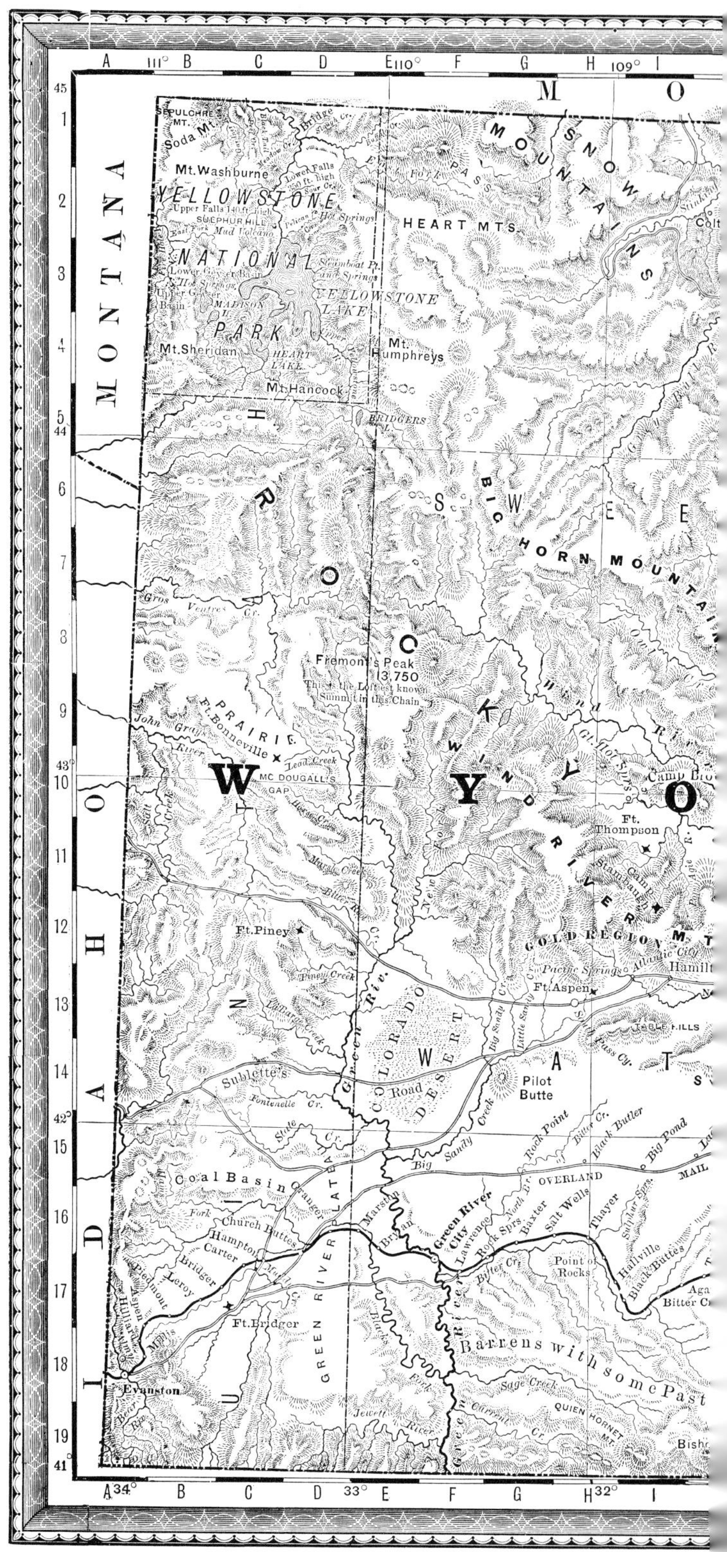

Areas in which Tom Horn was active as a stock detective are indicated by shading on this reproduction of an 1880 map of Wyoming.

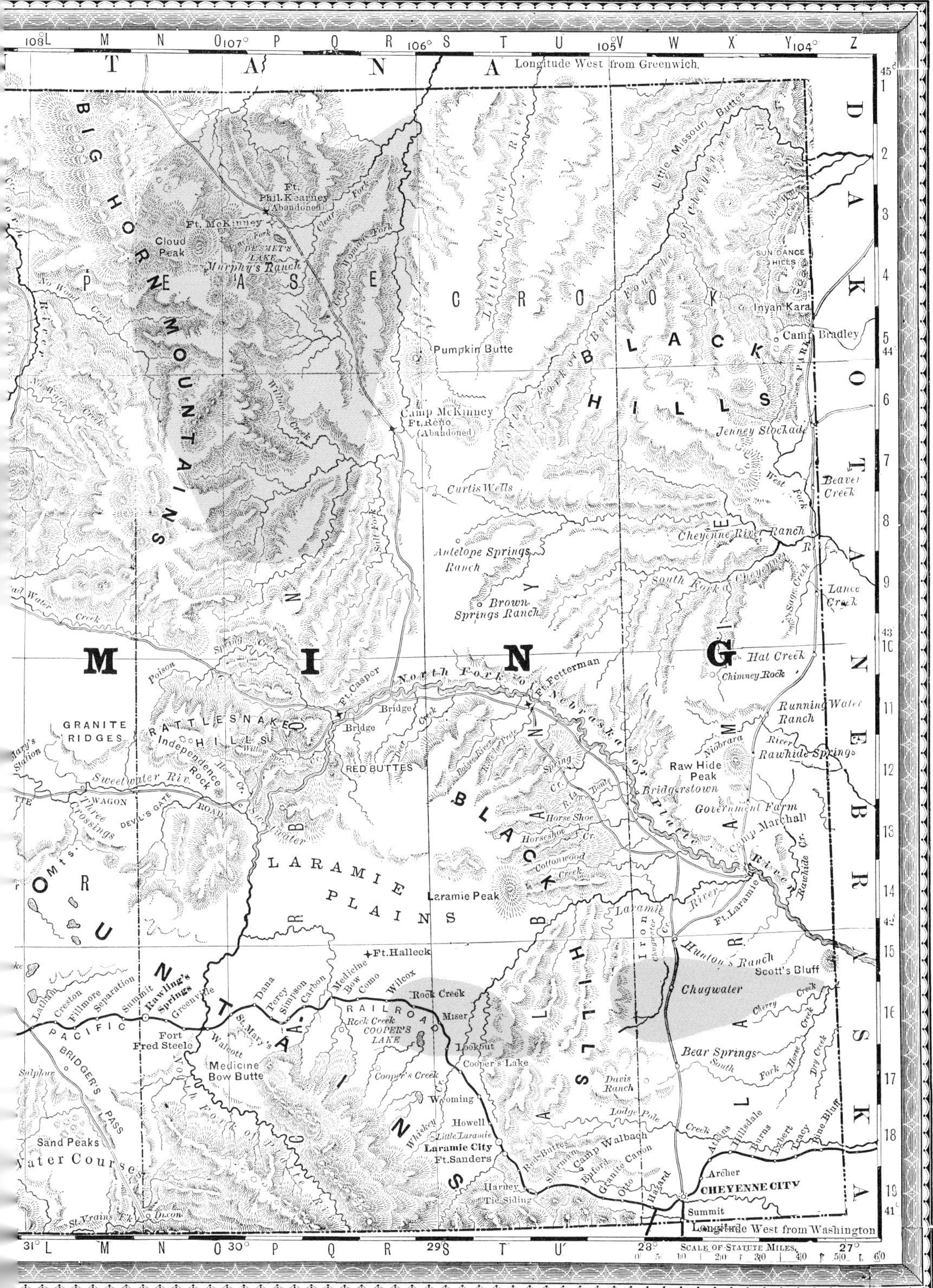
108° L M N O 107° P Q R S T U 106° V W X Y 104° Z
Longitude West from Greenwich.
M O N T A N A
D A K O T A
BIG HORN
Cloud Peak
Ft. Phil Kearney (Abandoned)
Ft. McKinney
Murphy's Ranch
DE SMET'S LAKE
PASSE
MOUNTAINS
Pumpkin Butte
CROOK
BLACK HILLS
Inyan Kara
Camp Bradley
SUN DANCE HILLS
Jenney Stockade
Camp McKinney
Ft. Reno (Abandoned)
Curtis Wells
Cheyenne River Ranch
Beaver Creek
Antelope Springs Ranch
South Fork of Cheyenne
Lance Creek
Brown Springs Ranch
M I N G
Hat Creek
Chimney Rock
Running Water Ranch
GRANITE RIDGES
RATTLESNAKE HILLS
Independence Rock
Ft. Casper
North Fork of
Bridge
Ft. Fetterman
Niobrara River
Rawhide Springs
Raw Hide Peak
Bridgerstown
Government Farm
Camp Marshall
RED BUTTES
Sweetwater Riv.
WAGON ROAD
Three Crossings
DEVIL'S GATE
Horse Shoe
Horseshoe Cr.
Cottonwood Creek
BLACK
HILLS
LARAMIE PLAINS
Laramie Peak
Ft. Laramie
Hartou's Ranch
Scott's Bluff
Ft. Halleck
Chugwater
Creston Fillmore Separation Summit Rawling's Springs
Greenville
Dana Percy Simpson Carbon
Medicine Bow
Como Wilcox
Rock Creek
PACIFIC RAILROAD
Fort Fred Steele
St. Mary's
Walcott
Rock Creek
COOPER'S LAKE
Miser
Lookout
Bear Springs
Davis Ranch
Medicine Bow Butte
Cooper's Creek
Cooper's Lake
Wyoming
Lodge Pole Creek
BRIDGER'S PASS
Sand Peaks
Howell
Little Laramie
Laramie City
Ft. Sanders
Camp Walbach
Hillsdale
Pine Bluff
St. Vrains Fk.
Dixon
Harney
Tie Siding
Buford
Granite Canon
Otto
Archer
CHEYENNE CITY
Summit
Longitude West from Washington
31° L M N O 30° P Q R 29° S T U 28° V W 27°
SCALE OF STATUTE MILES
NEBRASKA
LARAMIE

Longitude West from Greenwich.

transcribing and typing his shorthand notes. That finished document led to the issuance of a warrant for Horn's arrest, which was summarily carried out the next morning in the Inter-Ocean Hotel by three Cheyenne lawmen, including the sheriff, a deputy, and the chief of police. "Horn did not offer the slightest resistance . . . ."[46]

From the outset of his arrest, Horn was confident that he would never be convicted. Three reasons can be advanced for that optimism. First, Horn's former cattlemen employers would not allow him to be convicted for fear that he might incriminate them. Second, Horn was actually innocent of the crime. Lastly, perhaps it was Horn's personal conceit that he was in someway "above the law." But, such was not the case.

At the preliminary hearing on January 24, the packed court was stunned by the sensational disclosure of the "confession" as witnessed to by Snow and Ohnhaus. In addition, the prosecution introduced "pointing" circumstantial evidence which mandated "trial in the district Court for the death of Willie Nickell." Bail was denied over the strenuous objections of Defense Attorney Judge John W. Lacey, the Court holding "that the proof was evident and the presumption was great" against the defendant, an obvious prejudicial statement which set the tone of what was to come in the murder trial itself.

There is no question that at the time Horn's defense team represented "the 'legal brains' in the State of Wyoming." In addition to Judge Lacey, associate counsel included T.E. Burke, U.S. District Attorney for the District of Wyoming, and his partners, Edward T. Clark, R. A. Mason and T. Blake Kennedy, a New York lawyer from Syracuse, who had recently moved west. Who provided their fees leaves a lingering aura of suspicion that it was wealthy cattlemen, thus giving credence to their fear that Horn might talk when the chips were down. It was rumored that the defense fund exceeded half a million dollars. The undistinguished prosecution was headed by Walter R. Stoll, district attorney for Laramie County, and his associates, Clyde Watts and H. Waldo Moore.

In the months that dragged along until the trial commenced on October 7, Horn "was in daily conference with his attorneys." They proved a diligent team of defense lawyers, none better in the state. Their daily conferences only strengthened Horn's optimism about the outcome. During that drawn-out period, he was visited by a steady stream of friends and visitors and had all the comforts allowable under the circumstances, other than his personal freedom from behind bars.[47]

The trial opened on October 7 with the difficult selection process of a

Leslie Snow, then Deputy Sheriff of Laramie County, who was a witness to Horn's so-called confession. *Courtesy Wyoming State Museum.*

jury. Both prosecution and defense voiced comparable complaints about prospective jurors. After considerable argument, it was decided to make the selection by drawing from a list of 1,000 names in the presence of the respective attorneys and the judge. From the initial 36 names drawn, 12 were finally empaneled. Interestingly, the veniremen's occupations were rather lopsided: six were small ranchmen; one a cowboy and two ranch foremen for three small ranches; a blacksmith, butcher, and porter.[48]

A formal trial began on October 10 before Judge Richard H. Scott who arrived late for convening court into session. Some 100 witnesses had been summoned to testify, many under subpoena, many a reluctant witness at best. It was not until October 24 that the case was submitted to the jury for their deliberation.

The trial itself was highly detailed and probing. It need not be repeated here in full since a substantial part of the transcript has been conveniently published for anyone interested in pursuing the fine details.[49] Let it suffice to merely point out a few highlights which bear directly on the question of Horn's guilt or innocence.

First, a sensational media story which was played up in the press, even after Horn's death, needs to be dealt a mortal blow. Miss Kimmell was *not Horn's sweetheart.* Horn, himself, testified on three occasions (at the inquest, in the reputed LeFors "confession" and in Court) that he met the

71

Charles Ohnhaus, clerk of the federal court, who took down Horn's so-called confession. This photograph was taken some years after that 1901 event. *Courtesy Wyoming State Museum.*

lady schoolteacher for the first time when he called at the Miller ranch on his first and only visit there. Miss Kimmell destroyed her credibility at the inquest when she dramatically changed her testimony which had provided a solid alibi for the Millers to one that directly implicated them, a switch which certainly was to Horn's advantage.

In his recorded encounter with LeFors on January 12, Horn brought up the subject uninvited by the marshal of "the school marm." He divulged to the eager LeFors that:

> She was sure smooth people. She wrote me a letter as long as the Governor's message, telling me in detail everything asked by Stoll, the Prosecuting Attorney. Stoll thought I was going to prove an alibi, but I fooled him. I had a man on the outside keeping me in touch before I showed up with everything that was going on. I got this letter from the girl the day I got my summons to appear before the Coroner's inquest.
>
> LeFors dryly asked: "Did the school marm tell everything she knew?"

Horn, rather ungallantly replied,

> Yes, she did. I would not tell an individual like her anything; not me. She told me to look out for you. She said, "Look out for Joe LeFors; he is not all right. Look out for him; he is trying to find out something." I said, "What is there in the

72

LeFors matter?" She said Miller didn't like him, and said he would kill the S.O.B. if God would spare him long enough. There is nothing to those Millers. They are ignorant old jays. They can't even appreciate a good joke. The first time I met the girl was just before the killing of the kid. Everything you know dates from the killing of the kid.

To press the advantage, LeFors wanted to know, "How many days it was before the killing of the kid?" Horn replied, "Three or four days maybe. Damned if I want to remember the dates. She was there, and of course, we soon paired ourselves off." (The latter rather unsubtle inference led to the so-called sweetheart headlines.)

When LeFors asked about her nationality, Horn responded: "She was one-quarter Jap, one-half Korean, and the other German. She talks almost every language on the earth." And there he ended his comments on Miss Kimmell.

It may well be that Miss Kimmell's daily attendance at the trial sessions, coupled with her eloquent statement in Horn's defense, led journalists to believe that there was a romance between the two. The latter was reinforced by her last-hour appeal to the state governor for executive clemency.

Judge John W. Lacey who headed the defense team of lawyers for Horn. *Courtesy Wyoming State Museum.*

However, her prior flip-flop during the inquest, compounded by Horn's "confession," made Miss Kimmell an unreliable witness in the eyes of the law. This was an unfortunate state of affairs for Horn: had she been steady in her testimony in incriminating the Millers, Horn's fate might have fared differently.

As for trial highlights, three are notable. First, Horn's whereabouts on the day of the Nickell killing, July 19. External evidence was purely circumstantial. However, his "confession" was the only solid evidence to sustain the charge, other than some highly suspect witnesses' testimony. But there were three flaws to the prosecution's case in that respect. First, in his "confession," Horn stated that he had his boots off when he cut down the kid, supposedly so he could examine the body. He told LeFors that he was barefooted and ran across the terrain that way. The reason: there would be less evidence of boot marks. LeFors pointedly asked: "How did you get your boots on after cutting your feet?" To which Horn replied, "I generally have ten days to rest after a job of that kind." The jagged and rough soil and terrain, in and around the place where Willie was shot, would undoubtedly inflict considerable injury on barefeet which would take more than ten days to heal if one continued to wear boots and be physically active as Horn testified he was.[50]

A second flaw is in respect to the rock being placed under young Willie's head. Medical witnesses testified that this was probably due to the fact that when the boy hit the ground, he fell on his face and, as his life slipped away, he rolled over on his back. This would explain the dirt on his face (rather than being physically turned over by his assailant after he died), coupled with the fact that the immediate land environ was littered with gravel and numerous small rocks. Thus, at best, the rock under the head was geologically circumstantial.

Lastly, although Horn was on the open range after leaving the Miller ranch on July 18, making his way to Laramie, the prosecution made much of the fact, as had LeFors in the Horn-recorded conversation, that Horn traveled without food, other than a bit of bacon. The ability to live up to a week on little or no food for a man who weighed 202 pounds appeared incredulous to the prosecution. Horn argued to the contrary, since for years he had long practiced such abstinence on the open range.

The second highlight centered on the question of "a dark blue sweater covered with dirt and blood" left in a bundle by "a large dark man with slightly stooped shoulders" at a shoe store in Laramie shortly after Willie Nickell's death. When the man failed to reclaim the bundle, one of the proprietors opened it, making the discovery. After showing it to his partner, who recalled it was covered "with grass and gravel," it was laundered and worn several time thereafter. The color of the sweater was important since several witnesses cited it in identifying Horn while he was riding on the range in the vicinity of the Miller-Nickell ranches the day of the crime as well as the following day.

Another witness testified he ran across Horn on the road to Laramie and that his horse was sweating heavily and near exhaustion. He noted Horn's rifle and a bundle tied to the rear of the saddle. Unnoticed, he followed Horn into town and saw him enter the Elkhorn Livery Stable. The latter became another important element in the "tangible evidence" to establish Horn's exact arrival date in Laramie following the crime. Unfortunately, the stable's books, though produced and examined in court, failed to resolve that question.

Horn emphatically disputed this "tangible evidence" in respect to the sweater and bundle. He admitted he had a sweater, usually wore one, but he didn't have a blue one. Wrong color. As for the shoe shop and bundle, he had never visited one in Laramie, let alone left a bundle. Nor was he in the vicinity of the crime on the day in question.

A third noteworthy dimension of the trial was the introduction of testimony by a man from Denver who had seen Horn in that city at a saloon in the first week of October 1901. The witness testified that "Horn had done some boasting to the effect he was the 'main guy' in the killing of Willie Nickell." He further testified "that Horn had bragged about the Nickell shot being the best he ever made."

This testimony was buttressed by a second Denver witness who went further, saying he had got drunk with Horn. Under the influence of liquor, Horn "said he was the best rifle shot in the United States and the killing of Willie Nickell was the dirtiest piece of work he had ever done." But, the witness continued, the defendant "told him that lots of Cheyenne people were mixed up in the affair." The next day, according to the witness, Horn came to him and asked if he had talked too much, requesting that their conversation be kept silent.

A third Denver witness swore that Horn, when asked why he did not go after the reward money for the Nickell killing, replied: "Why that's all right, I'm the main guy in the case." Further, that the accused braggingly said: "That Nickell was the _______ best shot I ever made."

These three witnesses' testimony was seriously impeached by the established fact that during the first weeks of October Horn was in Denver's

Judge T. Blake Kennedy who was a member of Horn's legal defense team. *Courtesy Wyoming State Museum.*

At the left, T.E. Burke, U.S. District Attorney for Wyoming, who was one of Horn's defense lawyers. (RIGHT) Walter R. Stroll, District Attorney for Laramie County, the chief prosecutor in Horn's trial for murder. *Both Courtesy American Heritage Center.*

St. Luke's Hospital with a broken jaw. For three weeks, he "could not speak" because the fracture was immobilized in a plaster cast during his hospital stay.

The ultimate climax of the trial was Horn's testimony on the stand. The key defense ploy was to establish one singular fact, namely, the merit of his "confession" to LeFors. The transcript reads:

> Judge Lacey: Now, Mr. LeFors has said some things that you said to him, you may just explain to the jury what it was that you and LeFors were doing, when you had that talk with Joe LeFors that was overheard by Les Snow and Charlie Ohnhaus.
>
> Horn: We were just joshing one another, throwing bouquets at one another you might call it.
>
> Judge Lacey: What intention, if any, did you have in any way in the world to seriously admit that you had killed Willie Nickell?
>
> Horn: I never had anything to do with the killing of Willie Nickell; I never had any cause to kill him. And I never killed him. He was joshing me about it and I did not object.
>
> Judge Lacey: You did not object to the joshing?
>
> Horn: No sir.

The Cheyenne newspaper, commenting editorially on Horn's testimony. observed: "He gave his answers in clear, distinct tones, with a well-modulated voice, and the story he told was a straightforward tale that carried conviction to the minds of all who heard it."[51]

Horn, himself, made that abundantly clear to Prosecutor Stoll. Though admitting he made the statements to LeFors, he countered: ". . . I would have said anything else that pleased him. I felt very nice that morning; I felt peaceful, I would have told a dozen more lies if he felt inclined to think that way." As far as Tom was concerned, these were nothing but "Imaginary facts, that is all." He further countered, "I had been drinking considerably of course, but as far as that influenced anything I had to say, I knew perfectly well what I was saying."

In subsequent detailed and lengthy cross-examination by District Attorney Stoll, which took all day, Horn held his own. In respect to LeFors "confession," he reiterated time and again the motif that, "I thought I would sooner lie than disappoint him."

In the final redirect examination, Judge Lacey solicited a last response from Horn that closed the defense's case. In one response, Horn declared emphatically:

> Joe LeFors is the only man and the only man who tried or said in my presence that I had anything to do with the killing. Well, I am always of a rather generous

> disposition, I would rather lie than disappoint him; when he said I done the killing I
> would go along with Joe and other people like that.

Lacey probed one last time: "All the men that you ever did kill were these friendly talks with Joe and other people like that?" "As far as actual killing is concerned," Horn responsed, "I never killed a man in my life or a boy either."[52]

A major issue which went unresolved was the question of whether or not Horn was drinking or drunk at the time of his encounter with LeFors which lead to his "confession." In respect to this, the witnesses divided, half in the affirmative, half in the negative.

To strengthen the case for the prosecution, additional witnesses were called. Many of the previous and later witnesses for the state were either cowhands and/or small ranchers, all with a bias toward Horn, which was clearly noted on one or more occasions, even by the witnesses themselves. Two such telling witnesses swore they saw Horn's horses heavily lathered from hard riding on the day of and day after the Nickell killing.

To enhance the prosecution's case, LeFors returned to the stand and swore that on August 14, 1901, in the Vivolia Saloon in Cheyenne, he met Tom Horn at the bar. On bringing up the subject of the attempted slaying of Kel Nickell on August 4, Horn replied: "The shoot'n was done early in the morning, when the light was bad and the sun shone so on my sights that I could not fire well." Strange admission for a man who prided himself on his marksmanship, not to mention the fact that 13 shots were fired at Nickell in the attempt, three hitting their target.[53]

The prosecution closed its case on October 20. The following day Judge Scott instructed the jury. On the 22nd, Stoll made the arguments for the prosecution. He riddled the Laramie alibi that Horn went there on July 18-20 by discrediting the livery stable records, declaring them undependable. Drunk or sober, he argued, Horn knew what he was saying in Denver, which in essence corroborated what he had told LeFors. Lastly, Stoll lambasted the defense's expert medical witnesses and a gun maker who challenged the prosecution's contention that the victim was felled by two 30-30 Winchester rifle bullets. The following day Stoll's two associates added their brief measure to the summation for the state.

Then the defense opened its final arguments. Attorney Burke began with a powerful three-hour speech which slashingly attacked the state's case and submitted evidence. His argumentative thrust: doubt. He stressed the logic of Horn's alibi for July 18-20 and attempted to show that Horn

Judge Richard H. Scott who presided at Horn's
trial. *Courtesy American Heritage Center.*

had no motivation for the crime. As for the corroborating stories heard in
Denver saloons and the same told to LeFors, the answer was simple: "...
Denver papers copied the story from the Cheyenne papers . . . ." Thus the
Denver witnesses were merely repeating what they had read in the local
paper after the publication of the LeFors "confession" following the
January 24th preliminary hearing. Lastly, he defended the medical
opinions expressed.

Closing his remarks, Burke turned to the "confession." He declared: "A
confession must be seriously, willingly and purposefully made! And
statements to LeFors were not a confession! It was drawn out by the skill
of LeFors and was without purpose." To insure that end, he pointed out to
the jury patent absurdities and points raised by the prosecution. It was a
magnificent summation by a brilliant trial lawyer!

Concluding the defense's case was Judge Lacey. It was a "super-charged
address" along the lines of his colleague. An added touch was his address
to Horn's drunkeness or sobriety, humorously pointing out that he never
knew a drunken man who would admit to it. He held that Horn had been
"drinking all night before the alleged confession to LeFors. Although he
was not drunk, he must have been under the influence of alcohol." Time
running out, the court adjourned until the next day.

On October 23, Judge Lacey continued his summation, dissecting each and every facet of the state's case, hammering away at the circumstantial nature of the evidence and the "mere fitting of facts." He then turned to a close scrutiny of the witnesses called by the state, calling into account the testimony of two prime witnesses, suggesting outright that "they must have falsified [their testimony] as they conflicted." An orator of imminence, he closed the defense's case with an impassive appeal for acquittal and the life of Tom Horn.

Prosecutor Stoll had the final say. He ignored all of the defense's arguments in toto. Instead, he reiterated his earlier arguments. He shouted that the circumstances surrounding a confession did not matter "so long as it was a fact." Then, in a highly dramatic gesture, he picked up the jacket young Willie was wearing at the time of his death. He thrust his fingers through the bullet-torn holes and asserted: "The calibre, size of wounds and angle of the shots was of little importance—the fact that they were fatal is the paramount concern." (So much for expert witnesses!)

The last day of the trial, Stoll ripped into the defense unmercifully. He gave no quarter. A strategic ploy was to reconstruct the crime, step by step as the prosecution saw it, making Horn the villain. It was carefully presented, no link was left unforged. To cement that impression, Stoll turned to the Horn-LeFors correspondence which led to his eventual entrapment, thundering: "Tom Horn was not joshing in his conversations with Joe LeFors! These letters are conclusive evidence of his guilt!" He asked for a verdict of guilty of murder in the first degree!

At exactly 11:30 A.M., the jury filed out to commence their deliberations which lasted for the rest of the day. At 4:37 P.M., late that afternoon, they returned to render their verdict: Guilty! Judge Scott pronounced sentence: Horn was to be hung between 10:00 A.M. and 3:00 P.M. on January 9, 1903. The sheriff was instructed to see that the court's sentence was carried out. So ended the case of *The State of Wyoming vs. Tom Horn.*

Immediately, the defense team launched vigorous efforts for a new trial for a variety of technical reasons, including undue outside influence on the jury, as well as invoking a broad range of legal challenges. At best, these efforts only bought precious time, a whole year. In the interim, Horn was restive with his jail confinement and determined on an escape. A first effort was betrayed by an inmate he trusted, much to his anger and the chagrin of his hardworking lawyers. While the defense petition for a new trial was pending before the Wyoming State Supreme Court, Tom made good: he broke jail on Sunday afternoon, August 10, 1903. It was a bold

The Cheyenne courthouse where Horn's trial was held in October 1902.
Courtesy Wyoming State Museum.

and daring attempt, but foolhardy in the extreme. His vainglorious effort, fortunately without any casualty, resulted in a short-lived spurt of freedom. The alarm was sounded by Les Snow, firing his gun and shouting at the top of his lungs, which put Cheyenne on the lookout for the fresh fugitive. In no time at all, Horn was spotted in an alley just two blocks from the jail; he was overtaken and overpowered. Horn paid a heavy price not only for the earlier abortive effort, but also for the later brief successful escape interlude. It probably convinced a large segment of the population, notably the judicial community, that he was a guilty man. If he were innocent, then why run from the law? These escape efforts no doubt influenced the State Supreme Court to deny a new trial and to sustain the lower court verdict.

Although frustrated and embarrassed by their client's escape endeavors, the defense lawyers, under the circumstances, continued to work diligently, probing and gathering new evidence. One essential affidavit pointed a telling finger at James Miller; it was sworn to by a relative of the governor. Horn, himself, petitioned the governor on October 29, protesting his innocence.

A rear view of the Cheyenne courthouse and the attached jail. The circled X on the right is the courtroom; the circled X on the left is where Horn's jail cell was located. *Courtesy American Heritage Center.*

At a clemency hearing before the governor, lawyers Burke and Lacey made their case. Miss Kimmell also appeared at the behest of counsel, traveling from her home in Kansas City, in behalf of Horn. The state's case was made by the State Attorney General. Acting on the request of the state for like time in preparing its affidavits, the governor fixed the gubernatorial hearing on the early afternoon of November 5, later delaying it until November 12.

When Stoll heard of Miss Kimmell's affidavit, he was furious. He filed a perjury complaint against her in Cheyenne. She was summarily summoned to appear before the local Justice of the Peace on the afternoon of November 3. Defended by Burke, the peace justice refused to dismiss the complaint and ordered a bond of $2,000 for Miss Kimmell, a bond that was posted by two of Horn's friends, one being John Cole. A hearing was set for Saturday, November 4, at 10:00 A.M., to allow Stoll to make his case in person.

In all of the executive clemency maneuvering, Governor Fenimore Chatterton kept his counsel. On November 4, a large stack of affidavits in support of Horn were presented along with new evidence that implicated James Miller. That same evening the clerk for the District Court received a

Supreme Court mandate ordering Horn's execution to proceed on Friday November 20, between 9:00 A.M. and 3:00 P.M.

In the ensuing several days, a number of developments took place. One in particular is worth mentioning. A private meeting was held between the governor and Victor Miller, who had received a death threat. He was placed under police protection. At the same time, the number of cowboys frequenting Cheyenne was growing appreciably. A surreptitious note, with an ominous message "11-11-11," was tossed into the jail yard, and the lawmen took this to be a secret message to Horn that a breakout was in the works. To blunt that prospect, the sheriff enrolled additional armed guards to secure the courthouse from a forced entry to free the condemned man. In addition, the premises were well-lighted at night and declared off limits to loitering.

On November 10, Miss Kimmell felt the full sting of the law: a bench warrant was issued for her arrest on the charge of perjury. She had openly accused Victor Miller of the Nickell crime. Prosecutor Stoll was determined to bring her to trial in District Court. Under heavy bond, her case was scheduled for the week of November 23. It would begin three days after Horn's execution.[54]

The governor's formal hearing for clemency finally was held on November 12. It was a maze of contradictions and cross currents, not the least among them was a reputed "eye witness" to Horn's killing of the Nickell's boy! The Millers all executed affidavits protesting innocence, including solid alibis, which went unchallenged. To strengthen Miss Kimmell's credibility, long suspect and besmirched, Judge Lacey presented affidavits from a large number of citizens in Kansas City and St. Joseph, Missouri, which praised her solid character and her family. Though Lacey was no longer an active attorney for the defense, he still involved himself in the case because of his prior connection. He eloquently urged, "Governor, prevent an irrevocable wrong. Commute the sentence from death to life imprisonment, so that our client, when vindication came, might enjoy his liberty . . . ." A final affidavit was added to the defense's already large stack which bluntly pointed the finger of perjury at a central Denver witness.

All to no avail. The governor remained unconvinced. At 3:30 P.M., November 14, he made known his decision. There would be no reprieve, no commutation of sentence. Horn was to hang. None of the affidavits persuaded him, least of all Miss Kimmell's which he did not believe to be true. His reason for this was made clear: "My investigations have led me to believe that Miss Kimmell, at this stage of the proceedings, was willing to

The twelve-man jury that convicted Tom Horn of Willie Nickell's murder. *Courtesy Wyoming State Museum.*

present theories to save Horn, intending after the commutation of the sentence to exonerate Victor Miller of the insinuation cast upon him by her affidavit." Horn had little time left.

The last three days of Horn's earthly existence are perhaps the best documented of any of the days in his life before! On the morning of November 18, he received a tantalizing letter dated Laramie, November 17, unsigned. It read simply: "I killed Willie Nickell, tell them I do not want to see an innocent man hung. I will confess if they will not hang me." Horn dispatched it to his attorneys. To no avail.

That afternoon, he received the Cheyenne newspaper which had printed Governor Chatterton's final decision. Horn read it impassively. Handing the paper back to his jailer, he remarked: ". . . I guess I've reached the end of the trail. I'm not surprised at the Governor's decision, because the Courts had already attended to my case, but it does seem rather hard, after all. Well, I'm ready any time now. I'm not afraid to die."

84

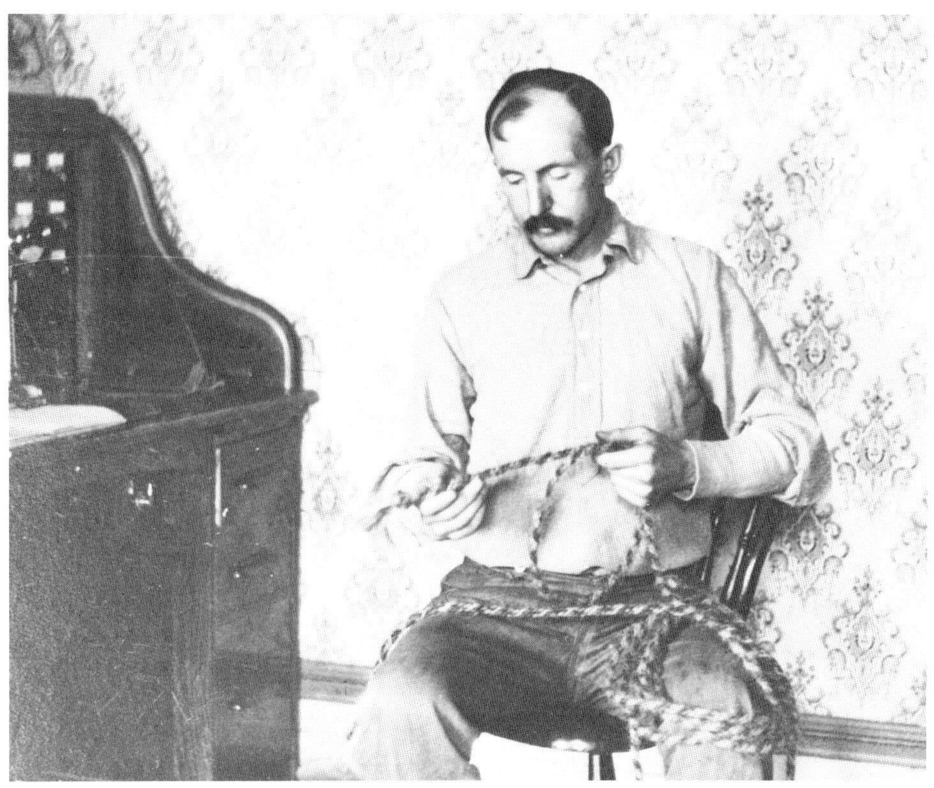

Horn in the jail office working on making one of his hackamores, a hobby that helped while away the tedious months of imprisonment. *Courtesy Wyoming State Museum.*

The next day, November 19, Horn prepared for death. He wrote some letters and began to make arrangements for the disbursement of his personal effects. While whiling away the tedious hours of long imprisonment, Tom had spent much of his time "making hair ropes, hackamores and leather bridles for his friends." He was an expert at making them. It helped fill the void. His second occupation was the writing of his autobiography. It was neatly written in pencil. He decided to give the latter, along with a few personal effects, to his longtime employer and devoted friend, John Coble.[55]

Even as the gallows were being built by James P. Julian, a Cheyenne architect, another startling affidavit was received in the late afternoon by Horn's lawyers. But time really had run out. Besides, the gallows were almost in place. It was "a classic in Rube Goldbergism." In essence, Horn would execute himself. Once he stepped on the trap, his weight would

Horn standing in the corridor of the jail where he was confined. Note his moustache has been shaved off. *Courtesy Wyoming State Museum.*

activate a spring which in turn would start a flow of water from one can to another. When the water level fell to the desired mark, a weight would knock out a support post and the trap would be sprung. All would be over in less than a minute, once the mechanism was set in motion by Horn's positioning on the trap.

During the last full day in Horn's life, his brother Charles arrived and made the necessary arrangements for the morrow. Coble arranged to purchase the best casket Cheyenne had to offer and paid for the funeral expenses. Horn's brother made burial arrangements to have the body returned to Boulder, Colorado, where he resided. Because of public sentiment, and in fear that the execution might be disrupted, Governor Chatterton called out a company of three troops of the State National Guard to secure and protect the Laramie County Courthouse. That night the building was a heavily armed beehive of men, both law and military.

At the conclusion of the day, Horn, after eating his dinner meal, was visited by the local clergymen: a Catholic priest; an Episcopal priest, who falsely claimed that Horn had accepted his faith and confessed the murder to

The crowds that gathered in Cheyenne on the day Tom Horn was hung, November 20, 1903. The view is looking east on West 18th Street. The brick building on the right is the Masonic Hall, still standing today. Note the uniformed National guards armed with rifles in the foreground. *Courtesy American Heritage Center.*

Governor Fenimore Chatterton who refused to grant executive clemency to Horn, thus clearing the way for his execution. *Courtesy Wyoming State Museum.*

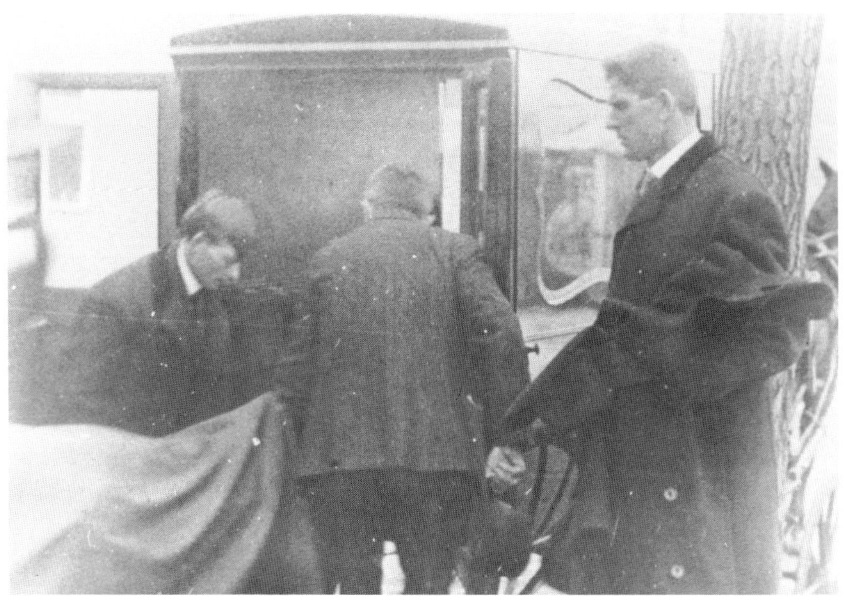

Horn's body being placed in the hearse after his execution. His brother
Charles is standing on the right. *Courtesy Wyoming State Museum.*

him; a Lovett Rockwell, joined by two lady singers, and Rev. Watson, the
Episcopalian, who sang to him after a short service. But these clerical
ministrations did not persuade Horn to religion. On the gallows, he was
asked, just minutes before his fall into eternity, had he accepted religion or
confessed. "No," was the crisp answer.

November 20 was Horn's final mortal day. He faced it calmly and
serenely. Not once was there any hint or trace of anxiety, fear or nervousness.
His deportment was cool and dignified. He was a man of steel, not to be
bent or dented by the prospect of death. As he approached the gallows, he
had requested that two of his stalwart friends sing a popular range song,
"Life Is Like a Mountain Railroad," in sonorous tenor voices. When asked
if he had anything to say, "No," was the quiet answer. As a clergyman read
prayers for the dying, "Horn, standing relaxed, listened without a tremor."
His coolness caused others to tremble. With a black hood over his head,
standing on the trap, the water trickling away his life in seconds, his last
words were to a friend who had recently gotten married. "I hope you're
doing well. Treat her right." The trap parted with a crash at 11:00 A.M., 31
seconds from the time Horn was placed on it. Unfortunately, the drop was
too short to break the neck, but, mercifully, the heavy-knotted noose knocked

88

Tom Horn was buried in the Columbia Cemetery in Boulder, Colorado, on November 22, 1903. The cemetery is located on Ninth Avenue and stretches from College Avenue to University Avenue. Some two-hundred yards west of Ninth and College stands the pink tombstone which marks his grave. He lies next to his brother Charles and his brother's wife, Elizabeth. The Boulder *Daily Camera*, November 23, 1903, took due notice of his burial. "The funeral of the late Tom Horn occurred from the Buchheit undertaking rooms Sunday afternoon and was largely attended from the outside. A respectful crowd heeded the admonition 'Funeral Private' posted on the door...A crowd followed the remains to the grave..." (The year 1861 is an error; it should read 1860.) *Courtesy American Heritage Center, University of Wyoming, Laramie.*

him unconscious. His pulse continued to beat for 17 minutes before death, at last, claimed him.[56]

The body was taken to the Gleason Mortuary and prepared for transport to Boulder, Colorado, escorted by Horn's brother Charles. On arrival in Boulder, Tom was buried "with all respect that relatives and friends could show." He had the "largest funeral that was ever in this town," according to brother Charles. "Everybody showed due courtesy to the hearse as it went seven blocks. They stood on the street with their hats off as we passed along," he wrote to Coble on November 27. Arriving at the cemetery, "there was hardly standing room. There must have been anyhow 2,500 people at the funeral."[57] The grave was marked by a polished granite headstone that simply read: IN LOVING MEMORY OF TOM HORN 1861-1903. (The birth year should read 1860.) He now belonged to history.

Three days before his execution, November 17, Horn wrote an important and perceptive letter to John Coble. In it he had some devastating things to say, thoughts which still cast long shadows:

> ... You know they can't hurt a Christian, and as I am prepared, it is all right ...
> I want you to always understand that the stenographic notes taken in the United States marshal's office were all changed to suit the occasion. The notes read at the trial were not the original notes at all. Everything of an incriminating nature read in those notes was manufactured and put in. It won't do any good to kick at that now, so let-er go ....

The governor's decision was no surprise to me, for I was tried, convicted and hung before I left the ranch. My famous confession was also made days before I came to town.

I told Burke to give you some writing I did; be sure and get it. You will not need anything to remember me by, but you will have that anyway ...

I won't need anything where I am going ....[58]

Horn's comments on the confession are provocative. In reading the entire transcript of that document, one is struck by the scatological structure of the conversation; it is higgly piggly, a mishmash without orderly development or even near completion of portions of the dialogue. Ohnhaus, the stenographer, testified in Court: " 'I took down the conversation one way. I didn't take it all . . . I took all I thought important and essential.' " Perhaps this may account for the meandering nature of the conversation. But Tom maintained to the end that the stenographic record was not accurate. Indeed, he wrote the young court reporter a plaintive letter from his jail cell, asking him to go to his "attorneys and tell them the whole truth . . . I am appealing to you for the truth only . . . and forever clear your mind and conscience of a burden that you will certainly find hard to bear through life, no matter how stout-hearted you may feel." He concluded his appeal with this sentence: "You were made a tool of some one, and now, for the last time, I ask you to tell only the truth." The plea fell on deaf ears.[59]

Second, because of the nature of Horn's reputation, it is probably a truism, he could not have received a fair and impartial trial in the milieu of Wyoming at the turn of the century. The struggle between the cattle barons and small ranchers, cowmen and sheepmen made that a certainty. As a friend remarked, "he was cruelly framed to the gallows by the rustlers and their friends . . . ." Another contemporary thought "Horn was the subject of a base conspiracy."[60]

LeFors, himself, gives eloquent testimony to the fact that Horn did not receive a fair trial. He later wrote: "Walter Stoll [the prosecutor] often stated *we must be careful in the trial of this case in order not to allow grounds for a reversal in case of a conviction and a new trial. For that reason much evidence was left out at Tom Horn's trial.*"[61] Certainly, the testimony of the cattleman known as "George," the liberated lady of questionable morals, and the unnamed lady detective, who witnessed her drunken revelations about Horn, never surfaced in the trial proceedings.[62]

On his final earthly day, Horn penned a last letter, ten minutes before he was to walk his last mile. Again, it was to John Coble. It was a reply to Coble's request for Horn to tell all he knew about the Nickell boy's killing.

In response, he recorded that the last night he stayed with the Millers, July 17, Jim Miller and a neighbor-friend, William McDonald, "opened the conversation by saying that he and Miller were going to kill off the Nickell outfit and wanted me to go in on it." There was pay in the offering as well. As for Horn, "I refused to have anything to do with them, as I was not interested in any way." The next morning, as he was taking his leave of the ranch, McDonald told him, " 'Well,' he said, 'we have made up our minds to wipe up the whole Nickell outfit.' " Horn rode off. When he reached the Iron Mountain Ranch, he "heard there of the boy being killed. I felt I was well out of the mix up."

Some six to eight weeks later, he returned to "that part of the country" and encountered McDonald and Miller who "were laughing and blowing to me about running and shooting the sheep of Nickell. I told them I did not want to hear of it at all, for I could see that McDonald wanted to tell me the whole scheme. They both gave me a laugh and said I was suspicioned of the whole thing." He then accused a key witness of lying that "I came into Laramie on the run Thursday, [he] just simply lied."

As for the confession, Horn declared:

> All that supposed confession in the United States marshal's office was prearranged, and everything that was sworn to by those fellows was a lie, made up before I came to Cheyenne. Of course, there was talk of the killing of the boy, but La Fors [*sic*] did all of it. I did not even make an admission, but allowed La Fors to make some insinuations.
>
> Ohnhaus, La Fors and Snow, and also Irwin, of Laramie, all swore to lies to fit the case.

He repudiated the slanderous language in the confession which impugned Coble's integrity, telling his friend, "Your name was not mentioned in the marshal's office." He closed his last letter with these two sentences: "This is the truth, as I am going to die in ten minutes. Thanking you for your kindness and continued goodness to me . . . ."[63]

Was this the whole truth and nothing but the truth? We have only Horn's word for it, a final word written in the shadow of the gallows and imminent death when he faced eternity.

Many of Horn's friends remained totally convinced of his innocence up to and beyond his death. All of them called into question the profanity and vulgarity of Horn's language, which was atypical of his conversation, "as he was very rarely profane and never vulgar, even when drunk."[64]

What then did him in? It was his complusive braggadocio. If one can believe Miss Kimmell, Horn had "carefully fostered" his reputation as a killer, "for as he used to say to his friends: 'That is my stock-in-trade.' "

Since nothing but fear restrained rustlers, Horn saw to it that his reputation was broadcasted widely and publicly. He would casually drop in on a suspect cattle thief and then "entertain the family by accounts of his experiences as a government scout, deputy sheriff and as a Pinkerton detective. These bloody tales would leave his auditors open-mouthed, and for days after his departure not a calf would be stolen in the neighborhood." Coble appreciated the reputation Horn had spun for himself. In a letter to his partner, Frank Bosler, July 16, 1900, Coble expressed his anxiety over any sheepmen's attempt at driving off their cattle, warning, "I will at once have them arrested. But they are scared to death," he continued, "are hiring all the six shooters and bad men they can find. I want Horn back here; *he will straighten them out by merely riding around.*"[65]

Horn's "habit of boasting when in a romancing mood was well known." Even the Cheyenne newpaper commented on that aspect of his character: "When drunk he had a habit of boasting of his prowess, and was prone to claim to have committed every murder of which he had heard. *Few people took his boasting seriously.*"[66] Thus, his "joshing" with LeFors was nothing more than usual for Horn, but the resultant stenographic record of that encounter in the marshal's office became the cornerstone of the prosecution's case. As Miss Kimmell observed, "After all has been said and done, why was he hung? The answer is: 'Because of a drunken talk.' " Yet, when "sober he was quiet in manner and modest, but that when he was drunk he was loquacious and boastful." The latter was due to his cowboy/ scout life. It was long a tradition that when gathered around campfires such men would spin fancy yarns, usually with only some slight semblance to truth. In the bargain, Horn was a born romancer. "He had an active imagination, a keen perception and a genius for language." Always truthful in everyday affairs, "if spinning a yarn would give pleasure, he was not one to let facts stand in the way."[67] Thus, Horn hung himself with his habitual bravado, a penchant for tall stories. You might say he talked himself to death![68]

After his arrest in January 1902, Horn became the focal point of what has been called "yellow journalism," particularly in Wyoming and Colorado. The press was unmerciless in handling every facet of his case. Only the Cheyenne *Daily Leader* offered what might be termed friendly coverage. As the months dragged on, the long delay before the trial, the trial itself, the defense's efforts for a new trial, Horn's abortive and short-lived escape, the gubernatorial clemency hearings, finally the execution and funeral—all these received steady print attention. But more. False stories galore sprung up like weeds in a cabbage patch, stories absurd and obscene. Such garbage was roundly condemned by Horn's friends. Miss Kimmell and Coble both labeled the press coverage as prejudicial and sensational. The journalistic coverage shrouded Horn in a cloak of myth and legend, true and untrue.[69] That legacy affected subsequent writers to turn their vitriol on Horn's southwestern years. But those who knew Horn well had nothing but praise for the man even in death.

In 1904 when John Coble decided to publish Horn's jail-written autobiography, he contacted Al Sieber, asking him to write for publication his opinion of Horn. Sieber responded with a statement from Arizona under date of April 7, 1904. The fundamental premise of that testimonial was set out at the beginning: "A more faithful and better worker or a more honorable man I never met in my life." Sieber later thundered:

> ... knowing him, as I do, and taking all into consideration, I can not, and will not, ever believe that Tom Horn was the man the papers tried to make the world believe he was. These words and sentiments can not be put too strong, for I can never believe that the jolly, jovial, honorable and whole-hearted Tom Horn I knew was a low-down miserable murderer.[70]

Another contemporary Arizona friend concurred. He posed the rhetorical question: "Is it conceivable that a man with Tom Horn's high record in Arizona and with the qualities which inspired in his employers and friends such a degree of liking and confidence could be guilty of shooting a boy of fourteen?"[71] Needless to say, Coble was "convinced, and I re-assert it to be true, that Tom Horn was guiltless of the crime for which he died." His attributes of "bravery, loyalty, generosity, and the countless kindly acts which marked his pathway through life," these would have to remain unwritten, unrecorded. As for Coble, "I am proud to say that he was my friend, always faithful and just. When can I hope to see such another!"[72]

When Horn's autobiography was published in Laramie in 1904, it was the third first-hand account put forth, up to that day, by an active participant in the Apache campaigns in the Southwest. It had been preceded by *The Personal Recollection of General Nelson A. Miles (1897)* and Colonel George A. Forsyth's *Thrilling Days in Army Life* (1900). Miles, in his memoirs, published in full Lieutenant Marion P. Maus' field account of the death of Captain Emmet Crawford, an action in which Horn played a prominent role as Crawford's head scout, an imbroglio that caused him to be wounded in the left arm.

What Maus has to say, apparently quoted approvingly by Miles, concerning this episode is basic to the discussion which follows. That January

9, 1886, episode is well described by Horn in his autobiography and elsewhere. Maus wrote in his official report: "I cannot commend too highly Mr. Horn, my chief of scouts; his gallant services deserve a reward which he has never received." As already noted, Miles was to write a comparable testimonial for Horn when he was on trial in Reno for reputedly robbing a faro dealer. As for Forysth, in his recollections, he devotes only one chapter to the 1883 Tupper-Loco fight in which he played a prominent role, but makes no mention at all of Horn.[73]

One of Horn's talents, which made him attractive for army employment at first, was not only his cowhand skills, but his ability to speak Spanish as well as having learned Apache. No less a person than General Crook commented that Horn "spoke Spanish well."[74] But much controversy has swirled around Horn's precise role in the Army. Al Sieber is emphatic on this matter. He states that "Tom went to work for me in the government pack train in 1882; he was with me and worked steady with me for three years." During those three years, they made a number of scouting expeditions together. Since Sieber needed the help of a man he could rely on, he "always placed Horn in charge; for it required a man of bravery, judgment and skill . . . ." When making side-scouting trips alone, Sieber "always place[d] Horn in charge of all Indian scouts left behind in camp. This required a man who was cool and had judgment to control and handle those scouts." When he made other side-scouting trips, taking a few pack animals, Sieber relates: "I ever made it a point to take Tom with me, as it very often required me to have a man that I could rely on in every way, as I oftentimes had to split my crowd after being out . . . ." In doing so, Sieber "would always put Horn in charge of one set of scouts, tell him where and the time to meet me, and what to do; and I never had him fail to obey my orders to perfection." Horn's performance was unthwarted: "No matter what came up—rain or snow, clouds or sunshine—Tom was there to meet me, and true to the trust."

Is it any wonder then, with the high opinion Sieber had of Tom's abilities as a scout and as a leader, that he took Horn with him in 1883 "into Mexico with General Crook," an expedition graphically recounted by Horn. This was Crook's first successful campaign to bring back the Chiricahua Apaches who had fled the White Mountain Reservation. "During that trip," Sieber remarked, "Horn proved himself a very valuable man to me on many occasions."

One aspect of that expedition, the negotiations with Geronimo, again related by Horn, found Horn, as he tells it, serving as interpreter, having been "pushed forward" for that role by Sieber. At the initial Geronimo encounter, Sieber warned Horn, " 'Take a knife, Tom; stand while you interpret; forget that you may not live another minute, and think only of the talk.' " During all the early stages of the negotiation, "Sieber was sure that the Americans all would be slain, and he kept his hand within his shirt where he had a revolver with which he meant to blow out Geronimo's brains at the first move that looked like violence."[75]

Yet, with Sieber's testimony ringing loud and clear, Horn is usually reduced to being a mere mule packer, always in back of the line of action.[76] If such was the case, then how is it Sieber would elect to take Horn with him in 1885, again after the Chiricahuas broke reservation and fled back to Mexico? This was the expedition led by Captain Crawford. During the initial phases, Sieber was Chief of Scouts, but on being called back by General Crook to the San Carlos Reservation, he "placed Horn in charge of my scouts with Captain Crawford, and he stayed in Mexico." Would Sieber have recommended a novice, untrained and inexperienced, to succeed him as Chief of Scouts, or would the Army approve a greenhorn novice for such a critical assignment? Hardly!

Although Crawford lost his life and Horn was wounded, Lieutenant Maus and Chief Scout Horn were able to bring a considerable body of hostiles back, including Geronimo, until thwarted by the sale of whiskey and mescal to the Indians near the border, causing them to change their minds and return to their mountain sanctuary.[77]

When Crook was replaced by Miles, the new commander continued to retain Horn as his Chief of Scouts. This led to Horn's involvement in the final tracking and surrender of Geronimo to Lieutenant Gatewood during the months in 1886 which occupied the Lawton-Wood expedition assigned to that task. Wood, in his field diary, provided glimpses of Horn in action, including an almost fatal river drowning in early August 1886. He records: "...Horn came very near going under, as although a big strong chap he had not done much swimming in rough water."

Wood also describes several short side-scouting forays which were bare bones operation. He wrote: ". . .We took no rations except a little coffee and salt; each man carried two belts of ammunition, and an extra pair of mocassins. No blankets or bedding taken. Everyone of our party was on foot."[78] This kind of field experience, no doubt, influenced Horn to adapt a similar method in his range detective work and a technique in respect to food which few could believe a man of his size could subsist on. Thus, his spartan nature was nurtured as a scout and continued as an attribute in his Wyoming days.

After Horn's death, perceptions of him began to alter, especially in regard to his army service in the Southwest. Two army officers in particular were scathing in their denunciation of Horn's autobiography. Britton Davis in *The Truth About Geronimo* (1919) had this to say:

> During the three years from May, 1882 to May, 1885 . . .there were no civilian employees in any way connected with the management of the Indians except Sieber, MacIntosh [*sic*], and Bowman. The reader can draw his own conclusions when he reads the historical romances of Tom, Bill, and Charley, if those romances refer to the periods I have mentioned. After the outbreak in May, 1885, other civilians were employed in various capacities connected with the hostiles. Of these I have no knowledge . . . .

Towards the end of his memoir, Davis turned directly to Horn in respect to the Crawford expedition, writing:

> Sieber started with the command, but was later recalled by the General, and Tom Horn, who had been taken along as Spanish interpreter, took his place as chief of scouts. Horn afterwards wrote a book, or had one written for him, extolling his experiences among the Apache. This, however, was the first time he had anything to do in any offical way with them, or was in the employ of the Government at all in connection with the management of Indians during my term of service—1882-85 inclusive. And other officers still living, who preceded me for several years on duty among these Indians, know nothing of his reputed connections with them during their time. I mention the matter only to refute some of the misleading trash that has been written and published of those times; most of it barefaced stealing credit due some other fellow.[79]

Thomas Cruse in *Apache Days and After* (1941) was equally vitriolic:

> . . . Horn assumed to himself experiences and exploits which were certainly not his. As Al Sieber's successor under Captain Crawford, he served for the first time in any official capacity in connection with military operations against the Apaches, or the management of those on reservations.

Cruse continued his heavy-handed criticism "to prevent the theft of honors by glory hunters" in these words:

> Summed up, then, in my years of service among and around the Apaches I never so much as heard of Tom Horn until he appeared in Crawford's command in late 1886. Other officers queried on the subject, who like myself knew everyone concerned with the Apache situation, and were like myself on the very ground mentioned by Horn as his field of glory, agree that December, 1886 marked his first employment as Army scout. But his services later were excellent.[80]

Cruse was particularly bitter because of Horn's account of the Battle of Big Dry Wash, his own claim to fame. A criticism picked up and amplified by Will C. Barnes, noted Arizona pioneer and self-appointed historian. He reduces Horn to "a packer in the pack-trains . . . if my memory serves me right." As for Horn's account: "His long yarn in his book telling of his presence at the Battle of Cibicue is an outrageous, barefaced lie from start to finish. I knew every solder, officer, packer and scout that took part in that fight . . . Horn was not with the command at any time." Cruse apparently concurred in this at least in writing to Barnes.[81]

How does one square these damning criticisms with Al Sieber's remarks? It should be pointed out that Sieber wrote his statement for John Coble as the latter was preparing Horn's manuscript for publication, thus, had not read the contents. Sieber, in effect, though solicited by Coble, was writing on his own. He closed his April 7, 1904, letter in this wise: "Now, sir, if this will be of any benefit, use it to suit yourself. *It is all facts to a letter.*"[82]

Another intimate in Arizona, Horace E. Dunlap, held to the view "that Scout Horn . . . [was] entitled to rank next to Al Sieber as one of the most valuable Indian scouts who served in the Apache campaigns." He opines that had Horn "sustained a mortal wound instead of a minor injury," while serving with Captain Crawford, "he would have undoubtedly have gained lasting renown." Then he pleaded: "Let us give him due credit for valiant service rendered to his government and to the people of the Southwest in helping to free them from the dread Apache scourge."[83]

Ace Daklugie, the son of Nidahi Apache Chief Juh, held little brief for the army officers who penned their recollections. In an interview, carefully written down by a reliable researcher, he had this to say:

> As books came out on the campaigns against the Apache I bought and read them. I learned of officers who got promotions, some to becoming brigadier generals, who gave honest and accurate accounts of their experiences in various conflicts. Some were sympathetic with the Indians. But some used their books to twist and distort the truth of the contemptible actions to secure promotions and the respect of the white people. Among these I classify Carr, Cruse, and Forsyth. They may have been able to deceive their commanding officers but the Indians know of what they were guilty and have only contempt for them.

Daklugie, who was educated at the Indian school at Carlisle, became an army scout at Fort Sill, Oklahoma, and was pensioned when he retired from active duty.[84]

There is much validity in Horn's autobiography.[85] Many a statement is true in essence, though sometimes the chronology is askew and there is an occasional slip in spelling of proper names. But the latter is understandable.

At the same time, it is also true, as one historian opined, that Horn "allowed his imagination to soar when relating his own exploits."[86] That, too, is understandable if one accepts the premise that Horn loved to embroider and embellish the truth, particularly in respect to himself. Thus, the combination of fact and fantasy blend in his autobiography, but it does make for exciting reading.[87] It deserves the appellation, a Western classic.

But some historians are a jaundiced lot, perhaps even fickle. On the one hand, they condemn Horn's book as unreliable or distorted, yet, cite it in their bibliography and use it as a primary source! It appears in book after book which deals with the Apache conflict in the 1880s in the Southwest, especially Arizona. A noted bibliographer of Western Americana books, attributes the authorship variously to Horn, himself; John Coble, his friend, or Hattie Louthan, a member of the family that owned the publishing firm, the Louthan Book Company in Laramie, that printed *The Life of Tom Horn.*[88]

The leading historian of the Apache campaigns invokes this suspicion in respect to Horn's narrative of the Crawford campaign. Since Horn was the only participant to write an account of that expedition (what of Maus' field report published in Miles memoirs?), it should be the best authority. Not so. The historian concludes that Horn's "account is so hopelessly inaccurate and untrue as to be virtually worthless. For example," he continues, "Horn, who has *an excellent memory for some things,* unaccountably confused Crook's and Miles' campaigns, lending weight to the theory that he did not write his 'autobiography' bearing his name." If the latter be true, then why would Horn leave to Coble "some writing I did; be sure and get it."[89]

In a subsequent book, the same historian changed his mind. He takes this view in citing *The Life of Tom Horn:* "In this book, which probably was heavily edited or rewritten from a draft Horn may have worked up while in prison, he describes the ensuing actions [the Tupper-Loco fight] in a way which gives little doubt of personal knowledge of them on his part, although he was not yet a scout as he claims to have been."[90] Sieber holds otherwise.

Setting aside the question of authorship of *The Life of Tom Horn* (the reader must decide that matter), there is an unimpeachable contemporary source for the Crawford campaign, the account by Lieutenant Marion P. Maus and one by Horn, himself. Both of these were carefully recorded and transmitted by a field reporter for the Los Angeles *Times,* Charles

Fletcher Lummis, destined for a renowned career as journalist/writer/ editor, assigned to cover the 1886 Apache campaign. Maus' statement was printed in the Los Angeles *Times,* May 9, 1886. Horn's wounding was witnessed by Lummis! He reported what happened in these words: "Mr. Horn jumped down off his rock, and grabbed his left arm. I asked him if he was hurt. He said yes." Fortunately, the ball passed through the fleshy part of the arm and did not shatter a bone. "The man who shot Mr. Horn was Miguel Carador [Mauricio Corredor], the Mexican commander. He was immediately killed."

Not content with this story, which appeared in the May 16, 1886 Los Angeles *Times,* Lummis included a statement from "Thomas Horn, interpreter, and Chief of Scouts . . . a manly and reliable Missourian." That narrative compares favorably with what Horn recaps in his autobiography.[91]

Even though voicing grave doubts as to the validity of Horn's autobiography, one historian makes no bones about Horn's service with the Lawton-Wood-Gatewood expedition which led to Geronimo's final surrender in 1886. He writes: "No writing I have seen gives Horn credit for the courageous, able work he did with the Lawton column; but he had the stuff of greatness if, lamentably, he had other less admirable qualities as well."[92] General Miles concurred in that view early on in his command when he succeeded Crook.[93] So much for historical ambivalence toward Horn.

Perhaps the most devastating charges leveled at Horn came from Charles A. Siringo, the famed "cowboy detective." That nickname should alert the reader to the fact that he was probably trying to protect the exclusiveness of that handle for himself, fearing it might also be applicable to Horn since both were contemporary Pinkerton agents. Siringo boldy declares that Horn was sent into Wyoming with a gang of gunmen to help start the Johnson County War. He writes:

> This war, from all accounts as told to me by Horn and others, was a murdering project of wealthy cattlemen to get rid of small ranchmen. Many cold blooded murders were committed . . . the world will never know how many blood-stained dollars Pinkerton's National Detective Agency received for their part in the disgraceful crime.

Siringo, who had surely read *The Life of Tom Horn,* for he includes biographical details found only in that book, then turns to the Reno episode during Horn's several years as a Pinkerton man, noting that he got the firm "in a bad hole," As he tells it:

> . . . He was on a secret operation in Reno, Nevada. One night, single handed, he
> held up and robbed a large gambling hall. One of the faro dealers recognized
> Horn's face when his mask was slightly raised. Next day he was arrested and
> thrown into jail.

In response to the arrest and charge, William A. Pinkerton sent a trusted assistant "to bring Horn home" to Denver. The reason for this course of action was because the agency "could not afford to let him go to the penitentiary after his noble (?) work in murdering men in the Johnson County war." "Soon after Horn's return to Denver," Siringo continues, "he told me all about the affair." It cost the agency "a 'bunch' of money" to free Horn!

Later, according to Siringo, William Pinkerton told him "that Horn was guilty of the crime, but that his people could not afford to let him go to the penitentiary while in their company. Thereafter he continued to draw his weekly salary, and he [Horn] told me that he was paid for his time while turning the trick and while lying in jail."

This version is totally false. Note, there is no mention of the two trials Horn stood in Reno and the final verdict of acquittal. Also, the reader should recall that the Reno affair took place in 1891, *a year before the Johnson County War!*

Not content with these bald-faced lies, Siringo then recounts a meeting in Denver after Horn left the agency and had moved to Wyoming. He describes how Horn related to him, in a saloon, the murder of two cowboys, one named Matt Rash. He tells how one was ambushed and the other coldly murdered in this manner:

> . . . The other man he killed in his own cabin, where he was camped alone.
> Horn rode up after dark and was invited by the cowboy to stay all night.
> Horn said that after eating supper he started to shoot the cowboy, but he finally
> concluded to wait until he had washed the dishes. Then when the last dish was
> wiped and put away, he pulled his Colts pistol and shot him dead, and slept in the
> cabin with the corpse all night.

Not content with this horror tale of callousness, Siringo could not leave well enough alone. Like a magpie, he could not resist capping that story with yet another, which as he said, "disgusted me more than this one." This tale was while Horn was an army scout in Arizona. It appears that after a battle encounter with the Apache, Horn, accompanied by three soldiers, rode over the battlefield, Then,

> . . . One of the soldiers noticed a live three-year-old baby upon its dead mother's
> breast trying to nurse. The soldier called his companions' attention to it. Then
> Horn said he remarked to the soldiers that he would fix the little brat. So he

spurred his horse up to the baby, and leaning over, put a bullet into the urchin's brain.

Commenting on Horn's trial and execution for the murder of Willie Nickell, Siringo could not resist paying his dubious respect to the man in this wise: "With all of Tom Horn's faults, he should have credit for dying game on the gallows and being true to his friends who had given him employment as a killer of men for many years."

Again, not content with this surfeit of condemnation, Siringo adds "that Horn killed 17 men since first going to work for Pinkerton agency." On a trip to New York, William Pinkerton confided to Siringo "that he could have saved the life of Tom Horn had it not been for the danger of the public learning that he had been one of their trusted detectives."[94]

Like all of Siringo's sensationalistic charges flung at the dead Horn, the latter is, like the rest, pure fabrication. As for the Pinkerton agency, the true story is far different.

Three years after Horn's death, Robert A. Pinkerton, William's brother and partner in the agency after their father's death, obtained a copy of *The Life of Tom Horn.* After reading it, he wrote one of the most detailed and informative accounts of Horn, which warrants full quotation. He declared:

I have always been sort of sore at myself that I did not look a little more thoroughly into Tom Horn's case, as since reading this book I have an idea he might have been innocent. I also gave a copy of the book to Mr. Knapp, one of the Jockey Club stewards and it has also made him doubtful as to whether Tom Horn was guilty.

Horn was a peculiar, unique Western character, a man seen frequently in the Indian fighting days. He was at one time in our employ, having come to us with good army references as a brave man and a first class scout and tracker. Also some references from some Western sheriffs which he gave me, certifying to his honesty and bravery. He remained with us for about five or six years. We used him principally to follow up rustlers, cattle and horse thieves, stage and holdup men. We found in Horn a most thorough plainsman and trailer; a man of unquestionable courage and good judgment in all that pertained to his class of work. He left our employ to enter the employ of a cattle company in Sweetwater County, Wyoming, as stock detective. This company had been having a great deal of trouble with rustlers. In trying to clear the company's range of rustlers, cattle thieves and undesirable characters, it finally came down to open war between the ranch owners and stock detectives, Horn on one side and the rustlers on the other. We only occasionally heard of Horn but there were rumors that he had been connected with the death of several rustlers. This was the condition of the affairs out there when he was arrested for the killing of that boy. Our managers at the time believed that Horn was guilty and recommended to me that we offer him no assistance but since reading his book I have had some doubts as to his guilt. If you find the book of sufficient interest I would like to get your views when we meet in the Spring. Knowing Horn as I did I would judge the language he used to be entirely his. He was not an educated man; just a common grade school education, such as he could pick up in the West but he had read considerable western literature and during the time he was with us when he had leisure to do so, I found him inclined to read fairly good books.[95]

Had the Pinkerton National Detective Agency entered Horn's case, the outcome might have been far different.

From the present persepective of criminal law, Horn's so-called confession, today, would be totally inadmissible in a court of law. His defense team tried to argue that very point, only to fail. As to the body of circumstantial evidence, why didn't the defense hire outside investigators to document Horn's account of his movements from July 18 through July 20? Was this part of a "conspiracy" quietly engineered by the cattle barons to see that Horn kept his silence? Why did the governor not grant executive clemency? Was it due to political reasons? Why didn't the defense team try more vigorously to impugn the obvious perjured testimony of a number of witnesses? Was Horn, in the final analysis, a victim of his inferiority complex which lead him to heavy drinking and unlicensed boasting? "In his struggle for recognition, [did] Horn develop a dual personality: one—a perfect gentleman, the other—a homicidal maniac?" Was he really "the Doctor Jekyll and Mr. Hyde of the rangeland?"[96] You, the reader, must decide: the verdict is yours.

As for history in general, Horn, as mentioned earlier, was a legend in his own time and continues as a legend today. Very few cowboys wind up with an entry in the *Dictionary of American Biography,* but Horn is one of them![97] Popular culture has long laid claim to his life and times, beginning with the famed John Ford motion picture classic, *Stagecoach* (1939), followed in that same year by *Geronimo* (Paramount). A second film devoted to that Apache war leader was made in 1950, the highly fictionalized *I Killed Geronimo.* A more sensitive portrayal of the Apaches was presented in *Walk the Proud Land* (1956) and with another Geronimo in 1962, starring Chuck Conners. A fascinating and sympathetic portrayal of Massai, Burt Lancaster played the role, came with *Apache* in 1964.[98]

The year 1979 might well be called the year of Tom Horn, since two major treatments were released. The first came in *Mr. Horn,* a Lorimar Production for CBS Television, scripted by William Goldman and starring David Carradine. The telefilm was shown nationwide, in two installments, on February 1 and 3. That same year, Steve McQueen produced and starred in his film, *Tom Horn,* his last cinematic appearance before his untimely death. In comparison, the telefilm is closer to the true story of Tom Horn. The film version centers on the years 1901-1903, and, from the Hollywood perspective, ends dramatically with a reenactment of his execution. It was less faithful to the true story than the Goldman script, although equally entertaining.

Knowing Horn, I suspect he would have been delighted in being immortalized on television and motion pictures. But to know his story best, one has to return to *The Life of Tom Horn,* his more enduring monument.

The last word on Horn belongs to one of the nation's great western writers, Eugene Manlove Rhodes. In a letter to an equally great western historian, Walter Prescott Webb, he had this to say:

> Knew about Tom Horn from the other side. But not enough. Interesting—most significant of the "American" traditions, the Americanism, the very existence of which is denied in that public opinion is overwhelmingly and deeply for Nate Champion: that it is eager to give Tom Horn a chance for his white alley. That is the love of justice as opposed to law—and it is ingrained in the character of the old stock....[99]

As enigmatic a statement as is the ending of *The Life of Tom Horn:* "And I think that since my coming here [to Wyoming] the yellow journal reporters are better equipped to write my history than am I, myself!"[100]

NOTES

1. Monaghan, *Last of the Badmen,* pp. 110-111.
2. Details are given in Clara T. Woody and Milton L. Schwartz, "War in Pleasant Valley: The Outbreak of Graham-Tewksbury Feud," *Journal of Arizona History,* 18 (Spring 1977): 43-68; Earle R. Forrest, *Arizona's Dark and Bloody Ground* (Caldwell, Idaho, 1936; rev. ed., 1952), which presents a full though flawed history, and Monaghan, *Last of the Badmen,* pp. 111-112. Also useful is Will C. Barnes, "The Pleasant Valley War: Its Genesis, History and Necrology," *Arizona Historical Review,* 4 (October 1931): 5-35, and Part II, "The Pleasant Valley War of 1887," *ibid.,* 4 (January 1932): 23-40. An excellent summary is presented in Wayne Gard, *Frontier Justice* (Norman, 1949), pp. 62-77.
3. *The Life of Tom Horn,* p. 317.
4. *Ibid.,* p. 317; Monaghan, *Last of the Badmen,* p. 112; Bill O'Neal, *Encylopedia of Western Gun-Fighters* (Norman, 1979), p. 149; Horace G. Dunlap, "Tom Horn, Chief of Scouts," *Arizona Historical Review,* 2 (April 1939): 83 (after Dunlap's name is this subtitle, "One Who Knew Him"); Sieber letter, dated April 7, 1904, in *Life of Tom Horn* (1964 ed.), pp. 270-271. Forrest, *Arizona's Dark and Bloody Ground* (1952 ed.), pp. 182, 188-190, concludes: "Horn was associated with the Tewksburys there is no doubt," and adds, "The full extent of his activities will never be known. . . . ." He also disputes Horn's claim that he was a deputy under O'Neill, and for that fact, under any lawman at the time.
5. When Horn, as will be detailed later on, was employed by the Pinkerton Detective Agency, he presented "some references from some Western sheriffs. . .certifying to his honesty and bravery." Robert Pinkerton to William Pinkerton, January 19, 1906, quoted in James D. Horan, *The Pinkertons: The Detective Dynasty That Made History* (New York, 1967), p. 380.
6. Monaghan, *Last of the Badmen,* p. 112. William H. Barnes, for four years an associate justice on the Arizona Territorial Supreme Court, stated in a July 22, 1891 affidavit: "I have known him [Horn] to be a man who has always aided the Officers, Marshal and Sheriff with enforcement of the law. . .[he] has always been called upon by the Officers of the law to aid them and he has rendered official service." Microfilm WA-89, Washoe County, Second Judicial District, Case No. 2832. (I am most grateful to Terry Conrad, Department of Special Collections, University of Nevada Library, Reno, for microprints of *The State of Nevada vs. Thomas H. Horn.*) Herinafter cited *Nevada vs. Horn.*
7. Monaghan, *Last of the Badmen,* p. 112; Dunlap, "Tom Horn," pp. 82-83; Thrapp, *Sieber,* p. 365 *note,* and depositions of D.H. Ming, E.A. Snow, and Bert Dunlap, July 22, 1891, in *Nevada vs. Horn.*
8. Dunlap, "Tom Horn," pp. 83-84; Monaghan, *Last of the Badmen,* pp. 112-113. Dunlap does not have Horn returning to Colorado with Shores, but being invited at a later date to join the agency. This would square with the aforementioned affidavits which have Horn leaving Dunlap's employ in May 1890. *Nevada vs. Horn.*
9. Horan, *The Pinkertons,* pp. 380-381.
10. Monaghan, *Last of the Badmen,* pp. 114-118, for the Reno incident. However, some of his data is incorrect in respect to various details.
11. *Daily Nevada State Journal,* April 10, 1891, p. 2, cl. 2, describes the Reno robbery. (I wish to express my gratitude to Ms. Carol C. Baker, Library Assistant, Nevada Historical Society, Reno, for xerox copies of the pertinent newpaper accounts that follow with the page and column numbers indicated.)
12. *Ibid.,* April 11, 1891, p. 3 cl. 1.
13. *Ibid.,* April 19, 1891, p. 3, cl, 4. The grand jury handed down its indictment on April 18. The first trial is reported in the July 15th issue, p. 2, cl. 2, and the results in the September 30th issue, p. 2, cl. 2.
14. *Ibid.,* September 30, 1891, p. 2, cls. 2-3.
15. *Ibid.,* October 1, 1891, p. 2, cls. 2-3.
16. *Ibid.,* October 2, 1891, p. 2, cls. 2-3.
17. *Life of Tom Horn,* p. 327.
18. Monaghan, *Last of the Badmen,* pp. 137-152, especially pp. 144-152.

19. A good summation is in Gard, *Frontier Justice,* pp. 121-145, and T.A. Larson, *History of Wyoming* (Lincoln, 1965), pp. 268-282. The classic account is in A.S. Mercer, *The Banditti of the Plains or the Cattlemen's Invasion of Wyoming in 1892 [The Crowning Infamy of the Ages]* (Norman, 1954), while Helena H. Smith, *The War on the Powder River* (New York, 1966), is definitive, wherein there is *no mention* of Horn's involvement.

20. Monaghan, *Last of the Badmen,* p. 147. The foremost Wyoming historian doubts Horn's 1892 involvement and holds to the view that he came to the state in 1894. Larson, *History of Wyoming,* p. 372. Horn testitifed in court that he came to Wyoming in 1894. Dean Krakel, *The Saga of Tom Horn* (Laramie, 1954) p. 137.

21. *Ibid.,* pp. 284-295, 314-319; Lewis L. Gould, *Wyoming: A Political History, 1868-1896* (New Haven, 1968), Chs. 6-9. (Ch. 6 is on the Johnson County War from the political perspective.)

22. Larry D. Ball, ed., " 'No Cure, No Pay': A Tom Horn Letter," *Journal of Arizona History,* 8 (Fall 1967): pp. 200-202.

23. Monaghan, *Last of the Badmen,* pp. 153-154.

24. Lamar, *Reader's Encyclopedia of the American West,* p. 513.

25. O'Neal, *Encyclopedia of Western Gun-Fighters,* p. 149.

26. Larson, *History of Wyoming,* p. 373.

27. O'Neal, *Encyclopedia of Western Gun-Fighters,* p. 149.

28. Krakel, *The Saga of Tom Horn,* p. 4.

29. Monaghan, *Last of the Badmen,* pp. 161-168. Dunlap, "Tom Horn," p. 84, relates that ". . .Maus, acting under orders from General Miles, took steps to locate Tom Horn [at the outset of the war] and presently he was ordered to report to Tampa, Florida, where he was made chief pack master." Information on the Spanish American War as to dates and data were derived from *Webster's Guide to American History* (Springfield, Mass., 1971), pp. 328, 330.

30. Larson, *History of Wyoming,* p. 373; Monaghan, *Last of the Badmen,* pp. 191-193. In testimony during the inquest into the Nickell homicide, Horn testified that Coble's ranch in Albany County "has been my home for a number of years." *The State of Wyoming vs. Tom Horn,* "Testimony at Coroner's Inquest," p. 283, Wyoming State Archives, Cheyenne (hereinafter cited *Horn Case*). (I am grateful to Roger Joyce, Research and Oral Historian, Wyoming State Archives, Museums & Historical Department, for his assitance in obtaining a xerox of the case.) As to closeness of the employee-employer relations between Horn and Coble, see his letters in 1964 autobiography edition, pp. 269-270, 275-280.

31. Miss Kimmell's testimony, *Horn Case,* p. 80.

32. Statement by Miss Kimmell as printed in the 1904 autobiography edition, pp. 249-250 (hereinafter cited Kimmell Statement); Krakel, *The Saga of Tom Horn,* p. 13 *note.* The autopsy report and doctors' finding are in *Horn Case,* pp. 4-9.

33. Kimmell Statement, p. 249.

34. Horn testimony, August 9, 1901, *Horn Case,* pp 282-300.

35. Kimmell Statement, pp. 250-252; Monaghan, *Last of the Badmen,* pp. 194-196. Miss Kimmell declares that Willie was shot once through the heart. The autopsy disputes that conclusion entirely. The coroner's testimony indicates that at the outset Miss Kimmell gave Victor Miller, a prime suspect, an alibi, then reversed herself, thus discrediting her testimony as a whole. (The latter is pointed out for readers in order to evaluate her overall testimony.) *Horn Case,* pp. 80-97, 355-375.

36. Krakel, *The Saga of Tom Horn,* pp. 20-21.

37. *Horn Case,* pp. 301-314.

38. Kimmell Statement, p. 251; Krakel, *The Saga of Tom Horn,* p. 22.

39. Kimmell Statement, p. 251.

40. Joe LeFors, *Wyoming Peace Officer* (Laramie, 1953), p. 131 (hereinafter cited *LeFors Story*). LeFors was born in Paris, Larmar County, Texas, in 1865. As a young man he rode for the Pony Express and became an expert cowhand. He settled in Wyoming in 1886 and entered law enforcement, his profession for the rest of his working years. He died in Buffalo, Wyoming, October 1, 1940.

41. Krakel, *The Saga of Tom Horn,* pp. 21-22 and *note.*

42. *LeFors Story,* p. 136. (Italics mine.)

43. *Ibid.,* pp. 137-138.

44. *Ibid.,* p. 140.

45. The letters in question are printed verbatim in Krakel, *The Saga of Tom Horn,* pp. 46-47, who is quoting the first in full from *LeFors Story* which omits the letters in the published version of 1953.

46. All of the foregoing details, including verbatim quotations, are found in Krakel, *The Saga of Tom Horn,* pp. 48-54, which reprints in full the "confession," also found in *LeFors Story,* pp. 140-145. The confession is reproduced in part in the 73 *The Pacific Reporter* (St. Paul, 1903), pp. 708-709.

This is the Wyoming State Supreme Court's decision in *Horn v. State* (which affirmed the verdict and set the execution date as November 20, 1903). *Ibid.,* pp. 705-729, for full text. One item needs to be flagged for the reader's attention: Tom, on the spot, *gives his exact age to the year, month and day.* Can you?

47. Krakel, *The Saga of Tom Horn,* pp. 57-59.

48. *Ibid.,* pp. 59-60 and *note.*

49. *Ibid.,* pp. 59-207. Subsequent details and quotes describing the trial are derived from this invaluable source. The full text of the original trial transcript is in the Wyoming State Archives. *LeFors Story* does not give any information in respect to the trial itself.

50. Charles C. Coe, *Juggling a Rope: Lariat Roping and Spinning Knots and Splices, Also the Truth About Tom Horn, "King of the Cowboys"* (Pendleton, Ore., 1927), p. 103, a friend contends that when Horn was hospitalized in early October in Denver with a broken jaw, "The doctor who undressed him and put him to bed testified at the trial 'that his feet showed no signs of ever having gone barefooted.' " Actually, there was even better evidence. A friend of Horn, who was drinking with him in Laramie on July 21, testified that Horn got so drunk he had to put him to bed. In taking off his boots and socks he saw no evidence at all of "bruises or cuts on his feet." Krakel, *The Saga of Tom Horn,* p. 92.

51. Quoted in Coe, *Juggling a Rope,* pp. 104-105.

52. Horn's testimony is reprinted in full in Krakel, *The Saga of Tom Horn,* pp. 103-117, 197, for the defense; pp. 135-197, for the prosecution.

53. Horn testified in the examination by the prosecutor that he had met LeFors at the saloon either on the night of August 14 or 15, but denied he had owned up to the Nickell killing. Krakel, *The Saga of Tom Horn,* pp. 175-176, 188-189. LeFors' own sequence of how he finally trapped Horn into the "confession" belies his August conversation as the tipoff for him. *LeFors Story,* pp. 136-140.

54. The case was postponed three times and finally dropped by the prosecutor, evidently fearing "that her further testimony might have a boomerang effect, and so concluded to leave well enough alone!" But Miss Kimmell had the last word. In the December 19, 1903 Cheyenne *Daily Leader* "she again made affidavit to the absolute truth of her testimony before the Governor [in the clemency proceeding]!" Coe, *Juggling a Rope,* p. 109.

55. *Ibid.,* pp. 107-108.

56. An eyewitness to the execution, John C. Thompson, 40 years later wrote his recollection of Horn's hanging. It was published in *The Denver Posse of the Westerners Brand Book,* 13 (Denver, 1957): 111 *et seq.* It is also quoted in part in Krakel, *The Saga of Tom Horn,* pp. 260-264. One thing is for sure, he died a brave man. The Cheyenne *Daily Leader* said it all: "No man ever faced the gallows more cooly and bravely. He went to his death as calmly as though such an occurrence was nothing unusual with him, and by his dauntless bearing made it much easier for the officials." Quoted in Coe, *Juggling a Rope,* p. 110.

57. *The Life of Tom Horn* (1964 ed.), p. 244. A guard, at Coble's request, was posted at the grave to prevent the body being stolen.

58. *Ibid.,* pp 240-241.

59. Quoted by Coe, *Juggling a Rope,* pp. 104-150. Horn qualifies this accusation in his testimony for the prosecutor, saying he believed the stenographer "took it down as accurately as he could, and he didn't make any mistakes that I know of. . . ." Krakel, *The Saga of Tom Horn,* p. 186. Also see *Horn v. State,* p. 709. However, there is something curious here. Right after he provided his answer, six typewritten lines in the original manuscript are torn and are illegible. Was this purposeful or accidental?

60. Coe, *Juggling a Rope,* p. 88; Frank W. Mulock to J.W. Lacey, Denver, October 5, 1903, printed in full in *The Life of Tom Horn* (1964 ed.), pp. 258-259.

61. *LeFors Story* omits this from the chapter on Horn, but it is published in Krakel, *The Saga of Tom Horn,* p. 50, wherein he reprints LeFors story from the manuscript. (Italics mine.)

62. As an aside, it would appear doubtful that any woman, even under the influence of alcohol, would talk so freely as LeFors suggests in the company of a completely strange lady, who was a detective, according to the marshal.

63. Printed in full in *The Life of Tom Horn* (1964 ed.), pp. 242-243.

64. Coe, *Juggling a Rope,* p. 102; Miss Kimmell's Statement, p. 254.

65. Miss Kimmell's Statement, p. 249; quoted in Krakel, *The Saga of Tom Horn,* p. 44. (Italics mine.)

66. Quoting the Cheyenne *Daily Leader* in Coe, *Juggling a Rope,* p. 102.

67. Miss Kimmell's Statement, pp. 261-262.

68. From a psychological perspective, it may well be that Horn suffered from an inferiority complex. This would explain his need for drink to compensate in order to "puff" himself up. It would also

explain his hyperbolical nature in manufacturing tall tales, making himself bigger in life than he actually was in reality.

69. *The Life of Tom Horn* (1964 ed.), pp. 262, 272-274.

70. *Ibid.,* pp. 269, 271 (hereinafter cited Sieber Statement).

71. Dunlap, "Tom Horn," p. 85.

72. *The Life of Tom Horn* (1964 ed.), p. 274.

73. Miles, *Personal Recollections,* p. 471. Maus also testifies to the fact that Horn spoke Spanish well. *Ibid.,* p. 458; Forsyth, *Thrilling Days,* pp. 79-121.

74. *Crook's Autobiography,* p. 260.

75. Sieber Statement, pp. 269-270. Dunlap, "Tom Horn," pp. 75-81, gives a lot of first-hand information on Horn's activities, 1883-1886 while in the Army. Dunlap was at Fort Apache at this time in the beef-contracting business. In affidavits in *Nevada vs. Horn* other details surfaced: 1881, a packer for the Army; 1884-1886, at San Carlos Reservation as "scout and cattle herder."

76. Thrapp, *Sieber,* p. 271, calls Horn a packer in the 1883 expedition, a clear contradiction of Sieber's Statement. Also, see his *Sieber,* p. 227 *note,* and *General Crook,* p. 128.

77. James H. McClintock, *Arizona, Prehistoric, Aboriginal, Pioneer, Modern. . .* (3 vols., Chicago, 1916), I:247. Horn tells a comparable tale so it may well be that McClintock took this from Horn, though there is no attribution. However, in II:615, he mentions Horn's book. Thrapp, *Conquest of Apacheria,* p. 289 and *notes,* is of the opinion that Horn was not at the 1883 conference with Geronimo, acting as interpreter, while Sieber says he was. Thrapp goes further: he labels Horn's narrative of this episode "fictious" and declares that "the veracity of Tom Horn. . .most assuredly has been discredited, abundantly." *Ibid,* pp. 299-300.

78. *Chasing Geronimo: The Journal of Leonard Wood, May-September, 1886,* ed. by Jack C. Lane (Albuquerque, 1970), pp. 57, 83, 87-102.

79. Davis, the *Truth About Geronimo,* pp. 37, 196-197. Thrapp, *Sieber,* p. 263 *note,* points out that Davis "must have excluded packers, who were always civilians, from his blanket statement." Thus, in no way does Sieber's statement that Horn went to work for the government in 1882 as a packer ring untrue. Packers were civilians, not military personnel.

80. Cruse, *Apache Days and After,* pp. 220-221.

81. Barnes, "The Apaches' Last Stand in Arizona: The Battle of the Big Dry Wash," pp. 58-59. Thrapp, though critical of Horn's reliability, questions whether Barnes, writing 50 years later, could recall 125 names "comprising a chance military expedition of which he was not even a member." Thrapp later adds that Horn writes "as if he had not only been in the thickest part of the battle, but practically won it singlehandedly." Then he grudgingly admits: "He had an accurate memory of the site, which is remarkable in view of the fact that he wrote his account 30 years before Cruse or others put their recollection down. . . ." *Sieber,* pp. 221 and 255 *notes.*

82. Sieber Statement, p. 271. (Italics mine.)

83. Dunlap, "Tom Horn," p. 85.

84. Eve Ball, "Cibicu, an Apache Interpretation," from an interview with Ace Daklugie, in Ray Brandes, ed., *Troopers West: Military and Indian Affairs on the American Frontier* (San Diego, 1970), pp. 121-133. The quote is found on page 132. Daklugie, born near Fort Bowie (?), 1874, died on April 14, 1955. His mother was a full sister of Geronimo; his father the feared war chief Juh. *Ibid.,* pp. 121-123.

85. This is attested to by one of Horn's sharpest critics, Dan L. Thrapp, for in his *Sieber,* he relies on Horn's autobiography as evidence for a number of occasions. See pages 229-230, 240, 251-252, 268 *note,* 328, 381.

86. Forrest, *Arizona's Dark and Bloody Ground* (1952 ed.), p. 188.

87. One sharp critic of Horn's book, Thrapp, *Sieber,* p. 35 *note* and p. 80 *note,* writes that his narrative "is always interesting, if usually unreliable. . . ."

88. Ramon F. Adams, *Six-Guns and Saddle Leather* (Norman, 1969), p. 311.

89. Thrapp, *Apacheria,* p. 339 *note* (italics mine); Horn to Coble, November 17, 1903, in *The Life of Tom Horn* (1964 ed.), p. 241.

90. Thrapp, *Crook,* p. 85 *note.* Also see the preface for Coble's editorial policy and remarks in *The Life of Tom Horn* (1904 ed.)

91. Dan L. Thrapp, ed., *Dateline Fort Bowie: Charles Fletcher Lummis Reports on the Apache War* (Norman, 1979), pp. 162-184, reprints in full the two dispatches of May 9 and 16, 1886. Horn's statement is on pages 181-183.

92. Thrapp, *Conquest of Apacheria,* p. 352 *note.*

93. Miles affidavit, *Nevada vs. Horn,* as reported in the Reno *Daily Nevada State Journal,* October 1, 1891, p. 2, cls. 2-3.

94. Charles A. Siringo, *Two Evil Isms: Pinkertonism and Anarchism* (Reprint of 1915 ed.; Austin, 1967),

pp. 44-48. Siringo also records Horn's employment by the agency as 1889 and compounds matters in respect to the Johnson County War by stating, falsely, that Frank Canton, one of the leaders of the invaders, was "Tom Horn's half-brother." *Ibid.,* pp. 44-45. In his *A Cowboy Detective, An Autobiography* (Chicago, 1912), pp. 233-234, Siringo calls Horn "Tom Corn" (typo?) and in only one place "Tom Horn." There is only one Horn reference and that is to a train crew that attempted to kill him. Had that been the case, "he would have avoided the trouble of being hung in disgrace. Besides, many lives which he snuffed out for pay, while acting as stock detective for the cattlemen of Wyoming, would have been saved." This is a very brief mention without any of the lurid stories which he wrote in the aforementioned book in 1915.
95. Letter dated January 19, 1906, quoted in Horan, *The Pinkertons,* pp. 382-383.
96. Krakel, *The Saga of Tom Horn,* p. 4.
97. His sketch is in volume 5: 236. There is also one in Lamar, *The Readers' Encyclopedia of the American West,* pp. 513-514.
98. George N. Fenin and William K. Everson, *The Western From Silents to Cinerama* (New York, 1962), *passim.*
99. W.H. Hutchinson, *A Bar Cross Man: The Life & Personal Writings of Eugene Manlove Rhodes* (Norman, 1956), p. 208. The letter is dated March 10, 1944.
100. *Life of Tom Horn,* p. 311.

Index

trespassing on Mexican soil, 26

Gatewood, Charles B., 2nd lieutenant, in 1883 Crook campaign, 28; joins Lawton's column in Mexico, 40; negotiates Geronimo's surrender, 42; mentioned, 95; photo of, 41

Geronimo, Chiricahua Apache leader, 15; meets Sieber in Terras Mountains, 19; surrenders to Crook, 32; negotiates second surrender to Crook, 39; flees, 40; surrenders to Gatewood, then Miles; exiled to Fort Marion, Florida, 42; mentioned, 95; films of his later life, 102

Gila County, scene of Pleasant Valley War, 49

Goldman, William, writes script for TV film, *Mr. Horn,* 102

Graham-Tewksbury Feud, leads to Pleasant Valley War, 47-49

Hale, Thomas C., Horn's alias in Reno, 51

Haley, Ora, Wyoming rancher, employs Horn, 58

Harrison, William H., U.S. president, approves use of U.S. Army cavalry in Johnson County War, 55

Hentig, Edmund C., captain, slain by renegade Apache scouts at Cibicu, 21

Historians, view of Horn, 97-98

Horn, Charles, Horn's brother, makes burial arrangements, 86, 89

Horn, The Life of, autobiography, evaluated, 98-99

Horn, Tom: autobiography, 5; birthplace and family, 9; leaves home, 11; railroad worker, then cowboy, 11; farms with brother Charles in Flint Hills, Kansas, then near Burrton; miner in Leadville, Colorado Territory; hired gun in Royal Gorge railroad dispute; travels Santa Fe Trail to New Mexico; stage driver for Overland Mail; moves to Arizona Territory, works for U.S. Army quartermaster as a drover, 12; driver for Overland Stage Company, 14; resides with Coyotero Apaches, 16-17; Works for Tully, Ochoa & DeLong Company, Tucson, as cattle agent, 17-18; not at Cibicu Creek fight, 22-23; makes Army debut as a packer in 1882, 23; at Tupper-Loco fight, 26; at Battle of Big Dry Wash Creek as a packer, 27; flawed view of his role at Cibicu and Big Dry Wash, 27; in 1883 Crook campaign, 28; reputed role in that campaign, 35; confuses Crook and Miles campaign, 35; becomes Chief of Scouts on Sieber's recommendation; with Crawford in pursuing Geronimo, 36; wounded by Mexican forces, 39; Chief of Scouts for Lawton's column in capture of Geronimo; accompanies Gatewood to contact Geronimo, 40; with Gatewood in negotiating Geronimo's surrender, 41; resumes civilian life, 43; kills Mexican lieutenant at a dance; employed by Chiricahua Cattle Company; mines at Tombstone, 47; role in Pleasant Valley War, 47, 49; employed by John Rhodes, Gila County, 49; kills 5 train robbers near Willcox as a deputy sheriff; sets record for roping and tying a steer; employed as ranch foreman by Ming and Jones; refused job in Cody's wild west show; employed by Bert Dunlop, Graham County, as ranch foreman; assists Sheriff "Doc" Shores in capture of horse thieves, 50; employed as an operator for the Pinkerton National Detective Agency, 51; arrested for robbing a Reno faro dealer, 51; two trials for same described, 52-54; acquitted, 54; disputed role in the Johnson County War, 54-56; employed by John Clay to work for his Swan Land & Cattle Company in Wyoming, 56; service in Spanish American War, 57-58; returns to Wyoming, 58-59; encounters Joseph LeFors, 64-66; details of Horn's confession, 66-70; arrested for murder of Willie Nickell, bail denied, 70; trial for murder of Willie Nickell, 70-80; attempted jail breaks, 81, 83; description of gallow's mechanisms that hanged Horn, 85-86; last hours described, 86-87; last letters quoted, 89-91; execution, 88-89; burial, 89; in death praised by others, 93-95; various views of Horn, 89-90; films about Horn, 102; photos of: Horn, 10; mother, 11; Horn, 48; his personal weapons, 67; trial jury, 84; Horn making hackamores in his jail cell, 85; Horn, 86; Horn's body in hearse, 88; tombstone in Boulder, Colorado, cemetery, 89

Maps: Horn's scouting domain, 30; Wyoming, 68-69

Mason, R.A., attorney, member Horn's murder trial defense team, 70

Massai, Apache brave, subject of film, *Apache,* 102

Maus, Marion P., lieutenant, with Crawford in pursuing Geronimo, 36; succeeds Crawford on his death, 39; field account praises Horn, 93, 95; photo of, 38

Maxon (Maxson), Mason M., colonel, testifies for Horn in Reno trial, 53

Meadows, "Arizona Charlie," 50

Memphis, Scotland County, Missouri, Horn born nearby, 9

Miles, Nelson A., brigadier general, assumes command of the Department of Arizona, 35, 40; strategy described; introduces heliograph, 40; meets Geronimo at Skelton Canyon, 42-43, 47; deposition in Horn's Reno trial, 51, 53, 54; autobiography praises Horn, 93-94, 99

Miller, August (Gus), son of James E. Miller, arrested, released in attack on Kels Nickell, 62

Miller, James E., rancher, feud with neighbor, Kels Nickell, 61; accused of Willie Nickell's death, 81-82, 83, 90

Miller, Victor (Vic), son of James Miller, arrested, released in attack on Kels Nickell, 62, 84; accused of Willie Nickell's death, 83

Ming, D.H., with partner E.A. Jones, employs Horn as ranch foreman, 50, 53

Monaghan, Jay, one of Horn's biographers, 54

Moore, H. Waldo, attorney, member of Horn's murder trial prosecution team, 70

Mr. Horn, a TV film of his life, 102

Nana, Apache chief, 15, 39

Natchez, Apache leader, surrenders with Geronimo; exiled to Fort Marion, Florida, 43

Na-ti-o-tish, leads a band of Apaches in breakout; trail taken described, 26; defeated by Chaffee, 27

Neal, John M., lieutenant, testifies for Horn in Reno trial, 53

Nickell, Kels P., rancher, father of William (Willie) Nickell, 59; feud with neighbor James Miller, 61; runs sheep on land; shot and badly wounded, 62

Nickell, William (Willie), 14-year-old murdered, 59, 61; photo of and scene where he was slain, 60

Noch-ay-del-klinne, Apache medicine man, slain at Cibicu Creek, 21

Ohnhaus, Charles, U.S. court reporter, records Horn's confession of Willie Nickell's death, 66; mentioned, 90, 91; photo of, 72

O'Neill, Bucky, sheriff, Yavapai County, 49, 50; meets Horn in Spanish American War, 58

Owens, Commodore Perry, sheriff, Apache County, 49

"Peaches," real name Tso-ay, taken prisoner, becomes scout for Crook, 28

Pedro, chief of Coyotero Apaches, 16, 17; photo, 17

Pinkerton, Robert A., brother of William, letter expressing opinion on Horn's guilt, quoted on, 100-101

Pinkerton, William A., superintendent of the Pinkerton National Detective Agency, testifies for Horn in Reno trial, 53

Pinkerton National Detective Agency, employs Horn as operator, 51

Pleasant Valley War, 47, 49

Quaife, Milo M., longtime editor of the *Lakeside Classics,* 5

This book was designed and edited by
Donald Duke of Golden West Books. Cover
design and paste-up was completed by
Siegfried G. Demke, the Corral's Publication
Editor. Cover production layout was by
Andrew Dagosta, a commercial artist. Type-
setting was by Ruth Rodgers of E & R Computer
Graphics, in 11 point Times Roman.
Printing of this book was by
Walsworth Publishing Company, Marceline,
Missouri. Cover typography by Dick Yale.